A Treatise of

Contributions

Shewing the nature and measures of crown-lands, assessements, customs, poll-moneys, lotteries, benevolence, penalties, monopolies, offices, tythes, raising of coins, harth-money, excize, &c.; with several intersperst discourses and digressions concerning warres, the church, universities, rents & purchases, usury & exchange, banks & lombards, registries for conveyances, beggars, ensurance, exportation of money [&] wool, free-ports, coins, housing, liberty of conscience, &c.; the same being frequently applied to the present state and affairs of Ireland.

Sir William PettY

Alpha Editions

This edition published in 2024

ISBN : 9789361475344

Design and Setting By
Alpha Editions
www.alphaedis.com
Email - info@alphaedis.com

As per information held with us this book is in Public Domain.
This book is a reproduction of an important historical work. Alpha Editions uses the best technology to reproduce historical work in the same manner it was first published to preserve its original nature. Any marks or number seen are left intentionally to preserve its true form.

Contents

THE PREFACE. ....- 1 -
CHAPTER. I. *Of the several sorts of Publick Charges.* ....- 4 -
CHAPTER. II. *Of the Causes which encrease and aggravate the several sorts of Publick Charges.* ....- 7 -
CHAPTER. III. *How the Causes of the unquiet bearing of Taxes may be lessened.* ....- 15 -
CHAPTER. IV. *Of the several wayes of Taxe, and first, of setting a part, a proportion of the whole Territory for Publick uses, in the nature of Crown Lands; and secondly, by way of Assessement, or Land-taxe.* ....- 20 -
CHAPTER. V. *Of Usury.* ....- 27 -
CHAPTER. VI. *Of Customs and Free Ports.* ....- 32 -
CHAPTER. VII. *Of Poll-money.* ....- 38 -
CHAPTER. VIII. *Of Lotteries.* ....- 40 -
CHAPTER. IX. *Of Benevolence.* ....- 41 -
CHAPTER. X. *Of Penalties.* ....- 43 -
CHAPTER. XI. *Of Monopolies and Offices.* ....- 49 -
CHAPTER. XII. *Of Tythes.* ....- 52 -
CHAPTER. XIII. *Of several smaller wayes of levying Money.* ....- 56 -
CHAPTER. XIV. *Of raising, depressing, or embasing of Money.* ....- 58 -
CHAPTER. XV. *Of Excize.* ....- 63 -

THE PREFACE.

Young and vain persons, though perhaps they marry not primarily and onely on purpose to get Children, much less to get such as may be fit for some one particular vocation; yet having Children, they dispose of them as well as they can according to their respective inclinations: Even so, although I wrote these sheets but to rid my head of so many troublesome conceits, and not to apply them to the use of any one particular People or Concernment; yet now they are born, and that their Birth happened to be about the time of the *Duke of Ormond's* going Lord Lieutenant into *Ireland*, I thought they might be as proper for the consideration of that place, as of any other, though perhaps of effect little enough in any.

Ireland is a place which must have so great an Army kept up in it, as may make the Irish desist from doing themselves or the English harm by their future Rebellions. And this great Army must occasion great and heavy Leavies upon a poor people and wasted Countrey; it is therefore not amiss that *Ireland* should understand the nature and measure of Taxes and Contributions.

2. The Parishes of *Ireland* do much want Regulation, by uniting and dividing them; so as to make them fit Enclosures wherein to plant the Gospel: wherefore what I have said as to the danger of supernumerary Ministers, may also be seasonable there, when the new Geograpy we expect of that Island shall have afforded means for the Regulation abovementioned.

3. The great plenty of *Ireland* will but undo it, unless a way be found for advantageous Exportations, the which will depend upon the due measure of Custom and Excize here treated on.

4. Since *Ireland* is under-peopled in the whole, and since the Government there can never be safe without chargeable Armies, until the major part of the Inhabitants be English, whether by carrying over these, or withdrawing the other; I think there can be no better encouragement to draw English thither, then to let them know, that the Kings Revenue being above **1. 10.** part of the whole Wealth, Rent, and Proceed of the Nation; that the Publick Charge in the next Age will be no more felt there then that of Tythes is here; and that as the Kings Revenue encreases, so the causes of his Expence will decrease proportionably, which is a double advantage.

6. The employing the Beggars in *England* about mending the High-wayes, and making Rivers Navigable will make the Wool and Cattle of *Ireland* vend the better.

7. The full understanding of the nature of Money, the effects of the various *species* of Coins, and of their uncertain values, as also of raising or embasing them, is a learning most proper for *Ireland*, which hath been lately much and often abused for the want of it.

8. Since Lands are worth but six or seven years purchase, and yet twenty years just cross the Channel, 'twere good the people of *Ireland* knew the reasons of it at a time when there is means of help.

Lastly, if any man hath any Notions which probably may be good for *Ireland*, he may with most advantage expose them to publick examination now, when the Duke of *Ormond* is Chief Governour: for,

1. His Grace knows that Countrey perfectly well, as well in times and matters of Peace as War, and understands the Interests as well of particular persons, as of all and every factions and parties struggling with each other in that Kingdom; understanding withall the state of *England*, and also of several Forreign Nations, with reference to *Ireland*.

2. His Grace hath given fresh demonstration of his care of an English Interest in *Ireland*, and of his wisdom in reconciling the several cross concernments there so far as the same is possible.

3. His Graces Estate in Lands there is the greatest that ever was in *Ireland*, and consequently he is out of the danger incident to those *Proreges*, against whom *Cambden* says, *Hibernia est semper querula*; there being no reason for ones getting more Land, who hath already the most of any.

4. Whereas some chief Governours who have gone into *Ireland*, chiefly to repair or raise fortunes, have withdrawn themselves again when their work hath been done, not abiding the clamors and complaints of the people afterwards: But his Grace hath given Hostages to that Nation for his good Government, and yet hath taken away aforehand all fears of the contrary.

5. His Grace dares do whatever he understands to be fitting, even to the doing of a single Subject Justice against a Confederate multitude; being above the sinister interpretations of the jealous and querulous; for his known Liberality and Magnificence shall ever keep him free from the clamor of the people, and his through-tried fidelity shall frustrate the force of any subdolous whisperings in the Ears of His Majesty.

6. His good acceptance of all ingenious endeavours, shall make the wise men of this Eastern *England* be led by his Star into *Ireland*, and there present him with their choicest advices, who can most judiciously select and apply them.

Lastly, this great Person takes the great Settlement in hand, when *Ireland* is as a white paper, when there sits a Parliament most affectionate to his Person, and capable of his Counsel, under a King curious as well as careful of

Reformation; and when there is opportunity, to pass into Positive Laws whatsoever is right reason and the Law of Nature.

Wherefore by applying those Notions unto *Ireland*, I think I have harped upon the right string, and have struck whilest the Iron is hot; by publishing them now, when, if ever at all, they be useful. I would now advertise the world, that I do not think I can mend it, and that I hold it best for every mans particular quiet, to let it *vadere sicut vult*; I know well, that *res nolunt male administrari*, and that (say I what I will or can) things will have their course, nor will nature be couzened: Wherefore what I have written (as I said before) was done but to ease and deliver my self, my head having been impregnated with these things by the daily talk I hear about advancing and regulating Trade, and by the murmurs about Taxes, &c. Now whether what I have said be contemned or cavilled at, I care not, being of the same minde about this, as some thriving men are concerning the profuseness of their Children; for as they take pleasure to get even what they believe will be afterwards pissed against the wall, so do I to write, what I suspect will signifie nothing: Wherefore the race being not to the swift, &c. but time and chance happening to all men, I leave the Judgement of the whole to the Candid, of whose correction I shall never be impatient.

CHAPTER. I.

Of the several sorts of Publick Charges.

The Publick Charges of a State, are, *That of its Defence* by Land and Sea, of its Peace at home and abroad, as also of its honourable vindication from the injuries of other States; all which we may call the Charge of the Militia, which commonly is in ordinary as great as any other Branch of the whole; but extraordinary, (that is, in time of War, or fear of War) is much the greatest.

2. Another branch of the Publick Charge is, the Maintenance of the Governours, Chief and Subordinate; I mean, such not onely as spend their whole time in the Execution of their respective Offices, but also who have spent much in fitting themselves as well with abilities to that end, as in begetting an opinion in their Superiours of such their ability and trustworthiness.

3. Which Maintenance of the Governours is to be in such a degree of plenty and splendour, as private Endeavours and Callings seldom reach unto: To the end, that such Governours may have the natural as well as the artificial Causes of Power to act with.

4. For if a great multitude of men should call one of their number King, unless this instituted Prince, appear in greater visible splendour then others, can reward those that obey and please him, and do the contrary to others; his Institution signifies little, even although he chance to have greater corporal or mental faculties, then any other of the number.

5. There be Offices which are but πάρεργα, as Sheriffs, Justices of the Peace, Constables, Churchwardens, &c. which men may attend without much prejudice to their ordinary wayes of livelihood, and for which the honour of being trusted, and the pleasure of being feared, hath been thought a competent Reward.

6. Unto this head, the Charge of the administring Justice may be referred, as well between man and man, as between the whole State or Commonalty and particular members of it; as well that of righting and punishing past injuries and crimes, as of preventing the same in time to come.

7. A third branch of the Publick Charge is, that of the *Pastorage of mens Souls*, and the guidance of their Consciences; which, one would think (because it respects another world, and but the particular interest of each man there) should not be a publick Charge in this: Nevertheless if we consider how easie

it is to elude the Laws of man, to commit unprovable crimes, to corrupt and divert Testimonies, to wrest the sense and meaning of the Laws, &c. there follows a necessity of contributing towards a publick Charge, wherewith to have men instructed in the Laws of God, that take notice of evil thoughts and designs, and much more of secret deeds, and that punisheth eternally in another world, what man can but slightly chastise in this.

8. Now those who labour in this publick Service, must also be maintained in a proportionable splendour; and must withall have the means to allure men with some kinde of reward, even in this life; forasmuch, as many heretofore followed even Christ himself but for the Loaves he gave them.

9. Another Branch is, the Charge of Schools and Universities, especially for so much as they teach above *Reading, Writing, and Arithmetick*; these being of particular use to every man, as being helps and substitutes of Memory and Reason, Reckoning being of the latter, as Writing and Reading are of the former, for whether Divinity, &c. ought to be made a private Trade, is to me a question.

10. 'Tis true, that Schools and Colledges are now for the most part but the Donations of particular men, or places where particular men spend their money and time upon their own private accounts; but no doubt it were not amiss, if the end of them were to furnish all imaginable helps unto the highest and fined Natural Wits, towards the discovery of Nature in all its operations; in which sense they ought to be a publick Charge: The which Wits should not be selected for that work, according to the fond conceits of their own Parents and Friends, (Crows that think their own Birds ever fairest) but rather by the approbation of others more impartial; such as they are, who pick from out of the Christians Children the ablest Instruments and Support of the Turkish Government. Of which Selections more hereafter.

11. Another Branch is, that of the *Maintenance of Orphans, found and exposed Children*, which also are Orphans; as also of Impotents of all sorts, and moreover such as want employment.

12. For the permitting of any to beg is a more chargeable way of maintaining them whom the law of Nature will not suffer to starve, where food may possibly be had: Besides, it is unjust to let any starve, when we think it just to limit the wages of the poor, so as they can lay up nothing against the time of their impotency and want of work.

13. A last Branch may be, the Charge of High-wayes, Navigable Rivers, Aquæducts, Bridges, Havens, and other things of universal good and concernment.

14. Other Branches may be thought on, which let other men either refer unto these, or adde over and above. For it suffices for my purpose to have for the present set down these the chief and most obvious of all the rest.

CHAPTER. II.

Of the Causes which encrease and aggravate the several sorts of Publick Charges.

Having thus spoken of the several sorts of Publick Charges, we shall next consider the Causes which encrease them both in general and in particular.

Among the general Causes is, First, the unwillingness of the people to pay them; arising from an opinion, that by delay and reluctancy they may wholly avoid them, with a suspition that what is imposed is too much, or that what is collected is embezelled or ill expended, or that it is unequally leavied and assessed. All these resolving into an unnecessary Charge to collect them, and of forcing their Prince to hardships towards the people.

2. Another Cause which aggravates Taxes is, the force of paying them in money at a certain time, and not in commodities, at the most convenient seasons.

3. Thirdly, Obscurities and doubts concerning the right of imposing.

4. Fourthly, Scarcity of Money, and Confusion of Coins.

5. Fifthly, Fewness of people, especially of Labourers and Artificers.

6. Sixthly, Ignorance of the numbers, Wealth and Trade of the people, causing a needless repetition of the charge and trouble of new additional Levies, in order to amend mistakes.

7. As to particulars. The Causes of encreasing the Military Charge are the same with those that encrease Wars, or fear of Wars, which are Forreign or Civil.

8. An Offensive Forreign War is caused by many, and those very various, secret, personal distastes coloured——with publick pretences; of which we can say nothing, but that the common encouragement unto them particularly here in *England* is a false opinion, that our Countrey is full peopled, or that if we wanted more Territory, we could take it with less charge from our neighbours, then purchase it from the *Americans*; and a mistake, that the greatness and glory of a Prince lyeth rather in the extent of his Territory, then in the number, art, and industry of his people, well united and governed. And moreover, that it is more glorious to take from others by fraud or rapine, then to gain ones self out of the bowels of the Earth and Sea.

9. Now those States are free from Forreign Offensive Wars (arising as abovesaid out of Personal and Private Causes) where the chief Governours Revenue is but small, and not sufficient to carry on such Wars, the which if

they happen to be begun, and so far carried on, as to want general Contributions, then those who have the power to impose them, do commonly enquire what private persons and Ends occasioned the War, and so fall upon the Authors, rather then contribute to the Effect; otherwise then to quench it.

10. Defensive Wars are caused from unpreparedness of the offended State for War, as when defective Stores are served into the Magazines by corrupt Officers at the rate of good; when Armies are falsely Mustered; when Souldiers are either Tenants or Servants to their Commanders, or else persons, who for their Crimes or Debts, want protection from Justice; when the Officers are ignorant of their business, and absent from their Commands; and withal afraid to punish, because unwilling to pay. Wherefore to be always in a posture of War at home, is the cheapest way to keep off War from abroad.

11. The causes of Civil Wars here in *Europe* proceed very much from Religion, *viz*. the punishing of Believers heterodox from the Authorized way, in publike and open places, before great multitudes of ignorant people, with loss of life, liberty, and limbs, rather then by well proportioned tolerable pecuniary mulcts, such as every conscientious Non-Conformist would gladly pay, and Hypocrites by refusing, discover themselves to be such.

12. Civil Wars are likewise caused by peoples fansying, that their own uneasie condition may be best remedied by an universal confusion; although indeed upon the upshot of such disorders they shall probably be in a worse, even although they survive and succeed, but more probably perish in the contest.

13. Moreover, the peoples believing that Forms of Government shall in a few years produce any considerable alteration as to the wealth of the Subject that the Form which is most ancient and present is not the best for the place; that any established family or person is not better then any new pretender, or even then the best Election that can be made; that Sovereignty is invisible, and that it is not certainly annexed unto some certain person or persons.

14. Causes of Civil War are also, that the Wealth of the Nation is in too few mens hands, and that no certain means are provided to keep all men from a necessity either to beg, or steal, or be Souldiers.

Moreover, the allowing Luxury in some, whilst others needlesly starve.

The dispensing of benefits upon casual and uncertain Motives, the giving vaste Emoluments to persons and parties of no certain visible merit. These are the things which cause animosities among the totter-headed multitude, who are the tinder that the sparks of a few Designers may easily inflame.

15. One Cause of Publick Charge in matters of Religion, is the not having changed the limits of Parishes and Cures with the Change of Religion from Popery, and with the Changes in Plantation and Trade. For now when the Ministers of the Gospel preach unto multitudes assembled in one place, may not Parishes be bigger? that is, may not Flocks be more numerous, then when every particular sheep was, as heretofore, drest and shorn three or four times *per annum* by Shrift. If there be in *England* and *Wales* but about five millions of people, what needs more then 5000. Parishes? that is 1000. Sheep under every Shepheard. Whereas in the middling Parishes of *London* there are about 5000. souls in each. Upon which account there needs be in *England* and *Wales* but a 1000. Parishes, whereas there are near 10000.

16. Now the saving of half the Parishes, would (reckoning the benefices one with another, but at 100*l. per Annum* a piece) save 500000*l*. Besides, when the number of Parochial Parsons were halved, then there would need but half the present number of Byshops, Deans and Chapters, Colledges and Cathedralls, which perhaps would amount to two or three hundred thousand pounds more: And yet the Church of God would be more regularly served then now, and that without prejudice to that sacred, ancient Order of Episcopacy, and the way of their Maintenance by Tythes; and all this in a method of greater Reformation and suitableness thereunto.

18. But suppose it be said, that in some wild Countreys, a thousand people do not live in a less scope of ground then of eight miles square. To which I answer, that there are few or no such places, the largest Parishes I know, being not more capacious then of three or four miles square, in which is no difficulty, for the people to meet once a week at some central place within that scope.

19. Moreover I say, that a Curate of small Learning, if of good life, and duly Ordained, may officiate in four Chappels of Ease every Sunday; and the Preacher, who indeed should be a person of Learning and Eloquence, may preach every other Sunday in every of the said Chappels, by preaching in two of them one day, and in the other two, the other day: And this with Catechizing, and Extra-Lectures upon the Week-dayes, would perform as much as now is performed, and as much as by the blessing of God is necessary to salvation; for the yoak of Christ is easie, and his burthen light.

20. But to put an end to this doubt; I affirm, that if England and Wales were cut out in parcels of three miles square, there would be found few above four thousand such, of which to make Parishes.

21. Now if it be said, that the Alienation of these Tythes is Sacriledge; I answer, that if the same be employed to defend the Church of God against the Turke and Pope, and the Nations who adhere to them, it is not at all; or

less, then to give **3. 4.** of the same to the Wives and Children of the Priests which were not in being when those allowances were set forth?

21. If I had not an abhorrence from propounding the lessening of the Church Means, I could say, that the retrenching part of each remaining Parsons Tythes and Emoluments, and leaving them for part, to the free Contributions of their Flocks, were a way to promote the Gospel, and to give less offence to such as think that their whole maintenance should be made in that manner.

22. I might also say, that forasmuch as there be more Males then Females in *England*, (the said disproportion *pro tanto* hindering procreation) that it were good for the Ministers to return to their Cælibat; or that none should be Ministers, whilst they were married, it being easie among five millions of people to finde out 5000. that could and would live single, that is, one in a thousand: And then our unmarried Parson might live as well with half, as now with the whole of his Benefice.

23. Alwayes provided, that though the number of Parishes, and the measure of Benefices were lessened, yet that the same ought to be done without dammage to the present Incumbents.

24. As for lessening the Charge of Offices relating to the Government and the Law, the same will consist in abolishing the superfluous, supernumerary, and antiquated; and withall, in retrenching the Fees of others, to what the labour, art, and trust of their respective employments do require. For there be many Offices wholly executed by Deputies for small wages, whereas the Masters of them have ten times as much, although they know nothing either of what is done, or ought to be done in the business.

25. Now such Surplusages as these should be either restored unto the people who gave them unto the King, at a time when those Fees made up but a just reward for the Officer; or else the King keeping them still might take them for so much toward the Publick Charge, but not give them away to stop the importunate suits of any particular person, in whom and in all his dependants, such benefits do but cause a laziness as to the true original gain of the Nation, and themselves in particular, together with a total negligence and ignorance of the publick good.

26. Many are the particulars that might be instanced of this kinde; but my aim not being to prejudice any man in particular, I descend no lower, wishing onely that there might be an universal Reformation of what length of time hath warped awry, in which case no particular men are to be troubled; for if all suffer, none suffers, and all men would be no poorer then now they are if they should lose half their Estates; nor would they be a whit the richer if the same were doubled, the *Ratio formalis* of Riches lying rather in proportion then quantity.

27. To lessen the charge of Universities, unto which I adde the Inns of Court, which is not much, were to lessen the number of the Students in Divinity, Law and Medicine, by lessening the use of those Professions.

Now having spoken already of Divinity, I come next to the Law, and say; that if Registers were kept of all mens Estates in Lands, and of all the Conveyances of, and Engagements upon them; and withal if publick Loan-Banks, Lombards, or Banks of Credit upon deposited money, Plate, Jewels, Cloth, Wooll, Silke, Leather, Linnen, Mettals, and other durable Commodities, were erected, I cannot apprehend how there could be above one tenth part of the Law-suits and Writings, as now there are.

28. And moreover, if by accompt of the people, of their Land and other wealth, the number of Lawyers and Scriveners were adjusted, I cannot conceive how their should remain above one hundredth part of what now are; forasmuch as I have heard some affirm, that there be now ten times as many as are even now necessary; and that there are now ten times as many Law-suits, as upon the abovementioned Reformation, there would be. It follows therefore, that upon the whole there would not need one in a hundred of the present number of Retainers to the Law, and Offices of Justice; the occasions as well of crimes as injuries being so much retrenched.

29. As for Physicians, it is not hard by the help of the observations which have been lately made upon the Bills of Mortality, to know how many are sick in *London* by the number of them that dye, and by the proportions of the City to finde out the same of the Countrey; and by both, by the advice of the learned Colledge of that Faculty to calculate how many Physicians were requisite for the whole Nation, and consequently, how many Students in that art to permit and encourage; and lastly, having calculated these numbers, to adoptate a proportion of Chyrurgeons, Apothecaries, and Nurses to them, and so by the whole to cut off and extinguish that infinite swarm of vain pretenders unto, and abusers of that God-like Faculty, which of all Secular Employments our Saviour himself after he began to preach engaged himself upon.

30. Moreover, if it were agreed, what number of Divines, Physicians, and Civilians (that is, of men bred in Universities) were requisite to the publick service? As suppose 13000. in the present way, and perhaps not above 6000. in that way of Retrenchment which we propound; then supposing that but one in forty dyes *per annum*, it follows that less then 350. might suffice to be sent yearly out of the Universities: Where supposing they stay five years one with another, it followeth also that about 1800. is the number of Students fit to be allowed in the Universities at a time; I mean, of such as intend to make Learning their Trade and way of Livelihood.

31. I might intimate, that if 1800. Students were enough, and that if there were 40000. Parish Children and Foundlings in *England*, it were probable that one in twenty of them might be of excellent wit and towardness.

Now since the Publick may dispose of these Children as they please, and since there is Maintenance in both Universities for above 1800. what if our Professors of Art were in this manner selected and educated? But of this but *in transitu*.

32. Hereunto may be added, that by reason of Loan Banks aforementioned, whereby the Credits and Estates of all Dealers may be known, and all the mysterious dangers of money prevented, and that by good Accompts of our growth, Manufacture, Consumption, and Importation, it might be known how many Merchants were able to mannage the Exchange of our superfluous Commodities with the same of other Countreys: And also how many Retailers are needful to make the subdistributions into every Village of this Nation, and to receive back their superfluities. Upon these grounds I presume a large proportion of these also might be retrenched, who properly and originally earn nothing from the Publick, being onely a kinde of Gamesters, that play with one another for the labours of the poor; yielding of themselves no fruit at all, otherwise then as veins and arteries, to distribute forth and back the blood and nutritive juyces of the Body Politick, namely the product of Husbandry and Manufacture.

33. Now if the numerous Offices and Fees relating to the Government, Law, and Church, and if the number of Divines, Lawyers, Physicians, Merchants, and Retailers were also lessened, all which do receive great wages for little work done to the Publick, with how much greater ease would common expences be defrayed? and with how much more equality would the same be assessed?

34. We enumerated six Branches of the Publick Charge, and have slightly spoken how four of them might be lessened; we come next to the other two Branches, whereof we shall rather recommend the augmentation.

The first of these two Branches I call, generally speaking, Care of the Poor, consisting of Receptacles for the aged, blinde, lame, &c. in health; Hospitals for noysome, chronical, curable and uncurable, inward and outward Diseases. With others for acute and contagious. Others for Orphans, sound and exposed Children; of which latter sort none should be refused, let the number be never so great, provided their names, families, and relations were well concealed: The choice of which Children being made at their being about eight or ten years old, might afford the King the fittest Instruments for all kinde of his Affairs, and be as firmly obliged to be his faithful servants as his own natural Children.

35. This is no new nor rare thing, onely the neglect of it in these Countreys, is rather to be esteemed a rare and new project: Nor is it unknown what excellent fruits there have been of this Institution, of which we shall say much more, upon another occasion hereafter.

36. When all helpless and impotent Persons were thus provided for, and the lazy and thievish restrained and punished by the Minister of Justice, it follows now, that we finde out certain constant Employments for all other indigent people, who labouring according to the Rules upon them, may require a sufficiency of food and raiment. Their Children also, (if small and impotent) as aforesaid, being provided for elsewhere.

37. But what shall these Employments be? I answer, such as were reckoned as the sixth Branch of the Publick Expence, *viz*. making all High-wayes so broad, firm, and eaven, as whereby the charge and tedium of travelling and Carriages may be greatly lessened. The cutting and scowring of Rivers into Navigable; the planting of usefull Trees for timber, delight, and fruit in convenient places.

The making of Bridges and Cawseys.

The working in Mines, Quarries, and Colleries.

The Manufactures of Iron, &c.

38. I pitch upon all these particulars, first, as works wanting in this Nation; secondly, as works of much labour, and little art; and thirdly, as introductive of new Trades into *England*, to supply that of Cloth, which we have almost totally lost.

In the next place it will be asked, who shall pay these men? I answer, every body; for if there be 1000. men in a Territory, and if 100. of these can raise necessary food and raiment for the whole 1000. If 200. more, make as much commodities, as other Nations will give either their commodities or money for, and if 400. more be employed in the ornaments, pleasure, and magnificence of the whole; if there be 200. Governours, Divines, Lawyers, Physicians, Merchants, and Retailers, making in all 900. the question is, since there is food enough for this supernumerary 100. also, how they should come by it? whether by begging, or by stealing; or whether they shall suffer themselves to starve, finding no fruit of their begging, or being taken in their stealing be put to death another way? Or whether they shall be given away to another Nation that will take them? I think 'tis plain, they ought neither to be starved, nor hanged, nor given away; now if they beg, they may pine for hunger to day, and be gorged and glutted to morrow, which will occasion

Diseases and evil habits, the same may be said of stealing; moreover, perhaps they may get either by begging or stealing more then will suffice them, which will for ever after indispose them to labour, even upon the greatest occasion which may suddenly and unexpectedly happen.

39. For all these Reasons, it will be certainly the safer way to afford them the superfluity which would otherwise be lost and wasted, or wantonly spent: Or in case there be no overplus, then 'tis fit to retrench a little from the delicacy of others feeding in quantity or quality; few men spending less then double of what might suffice them as to the bare necessities of nature.

40. Now as to the work of these supernumeraries, let it be without expence of Foreign Commodities, and then 'tis no matter if it be employed to build a useless Pyramid upon *Salisbury Plain*, bring the Stones at *Stonehenge* to *Tower-Hill*, or the like; for at worst this would keep their mindes to discipline and obedience, and their bodies to a patience of more profitable labours when need shall require it.

41. In the next place, as an instance of the usefulness of what hath been propounded, I ask what benefit will the mending of High-wayes, the building of Bridges and Cawseys, with making of Rivers navigable produce, besides the pleasure and beauty of them? To which I also answer, as an instance of the premises, that the same, together with the numerous millions of Cattle and Sheep out of *Ireland*, shall produce a vaste superfluity of English Horses, the which because they have the many excellent qualities of beauty, strength, courage, swiftness, and patience concentrated in them, beyond the Horses of other places, would be a very vendible Commodity all over *Europe*; and such as depending upon the intrinsick nature of the English Soyle could not be counterfeited, nor taken away by others. Moreover, an Horse is such a Commodity as will carry both himself and his Merchant to the Market, be the same never so distant.

CHAPTER. III.

How the Causes of the unquiet bearing of Taxes may be lessened.

We have slightly gone through all the six Branches of the Publick Charge, and have (though imperfectly and in haste) shewn what would encrease, and what would abate them.

We come next to take away some of the general Causes of the unquiet bearing of Taxes, and yielding to Contributions, *viz.*

2. 1. That the people think, the Sovereign askes more then he needs. To which we answer, 1. That if the Sovereign were sure to have what he wanted in due time, it were his own great dammage to draw away the money out of his Subjects hands, who by trade increase it, and to hoard it up in his own Coffers, where 'tis of no use even to himself, but lyable to be begged or vainly expended.

3. 2. Let the Tax be never so great, if it be proportionable unto all, then no man suffers the loss of any Riches by it. For men (as we said but now) if the Estates of them all were either halfed or doubled, would in both cases remain equally rich. For they would each man have his former state, dignity, and degree; and moreover, the Money leavied not going out of the Nation, the same also would remain as rich in comparison of any other Nation; onely the Riches of the Prince and People would differ for a little while, namely, until the money leavied from some, were again refunded upon the same, or other persons that paid it: In which case every man also should have his chance and opportunity to be made the better or worse by the new distribution; or if he lost by one, yet to gain by another.

4. 3. Now that which angers men most, is to be taxed above their Neighbours. To which I answer, that many times these surmizes are mistakes, many times they are chances, which in the next Tax may run more favourable; and if they be by design, yet it cannot be imagined, that it was by design of the Sovereign, but of some temporary Assessor, whose turn it may be to receive the *Talio* upon the next occasion from the very man he has wronged.

5. 4. Men repine much, if they think the money leavyed will be expended on Entertainments, magnificent Shews, triumphal Arches, &c. To which I answer, that the same is a refunding the said moneys to the Tradesmen who work upon those things; which Trades though they seem vain and onely of ornament, yet they refund presently to the most useful; namely, to Brewers, Bakers, Taylours, Shoemakers, &c. Moreover, the Prince hath no more pleasure in these Shews and Entertainments then 100000. others of his

meanest Subjects have, whom, for all their grumbling, we see to travel many miles to be spectators of these mistaken and distasted vanities.

6. 5. The people often complain, that the King bestows the money he raises from the people upon his Favourites: To which we answer; that what is given to Favourites, may at the next step or transmigration, come into our own hands, or theirs unto whom we wish well, and think do deserve it.

7. Secondly, as this man is a Favourite to day, so another, or our selves, may be hereafter; favour being of a very slippery and moveable nature, and not such a thing as we need much to envy; for the same way that——leads up an hill, leads also down the same. Besides, there is nothing in the Lawes or Customes of *England*, which excludes any the meanest mans Childe, from arriving to the highest Offices in this Kingdom, much less debars him from the Personall kindness of his Prince.

8. All these imaginations (whereunto the vulgar heads are subject) do cause a backwardness to pay, and that necessitates the Prince to severity. Now this lighting upon some poor, though stubborn, stiff-necked Refuser, charged with Wife and Children, gives the credulous great occasion to complain of Oppression, and breeds ill blood as to all other matters; feeding the ill humours already in being.

9. 6. Ignorance of the Number, Trade, and Wealth of the people, is often the reason why the said people are needlesly troubled, viz. with the double charge and vexation of two, or many Levies, when one might have served: Examples whereof have been seen in late Poll-moneys; in which (by reason of not knowing the state of the people, *viz.* how many there were of each Taxable sort, and the want of sensible markes whereby to rate men, and the confounding of Estates with Titles and Offices) great mistakes were committed.

10. Besides, for not knowing the Wealth of the people, the Prince knows not what they can bear; and for not knowing the Trade, he can make no Judgment of the proper season when to demand his Exhibitions.

11. 7. Obscurities and doubts, about the right of imposing, hath been the cause of great and ugly Reluctancies in the people, and of Involuntary Severities in the Prince; an eminent Example whereof was the Ship-money, no small cause of twenty years calamity to the whole Kingdom.

12. 8. Fewness of people, is real poverty; and a Nation wherein are Eight Millions of people, are more then twice as rich as the same scope of Land wherein are but Four; For the same Governours which are the great charge, may serve near as well, for the greater, as the lesser number.

13. Secondly, If the people be so few, as that they can live, *Ex sponte Creatii*, or with little labour, such as is Grazing, &c., they become wholly without Art. No man that will not exercise his hands, being able to endure the tortures of the mind, which much thoughtfulness doth occasion.

14. 9. Scarcity of money, is another cause of the bad payment of Taxes; for if we consider, that of all the wealth of this Nation, *viz*. Lands, Housing, Shipping, Commodities, Furniture, Plate, and Money, that scarce one part of an hundred is Coin; and that perhaps there is scarce six millions of Pounds now in *England*, that is but twenty shillings a head for every head in the Nation. We may easily judge, how difficult it is for men of competent estates, to pay a Summe of money on a sudden; which if they cannot compass, Severities, and Charges ensue; and that with reason, though unluckie enough, it being more tolerable to undoe one particular Member, then to endanger the whole, notwithstanding indeed it be more tolerable for one particular Member to be undone with the whole, then alone.

15. 10. It seems somewhat hard, that all Taxes should be paid in money, viz., (when the King hath occasion to Victual his Ships at *Portsmouth*) that Fat Oxen, and Corn should not be received in kind, but that Farmers must first carry their Corn perhaps ten Miles to sell, and turn into money; which being paid to the King, is again reconverted into Corn, fetcht many miles further.

16. Moreover, the Farmer for haste is forced to under-sell his Corn, and the King for haste likewise, is forced to over-buy his provisions. Whereas the paying in kinde, *Pro Hic & Nunc*, would lessen a considerable grievance to the poor people.

17. The next confederation shall be of the consequences, and effects of too great a Tax, not in respect of particular men, of which we have spoken before, but to the whole people in general: To which I say, that there is a certain measure, and proportion of money requisite to drive the trade of a Nation, more or less then which would prejudice the same. Just as there is a certain proportion of Farthings necessary in a small retail Trade, to change silver money, and to even such reckonings as cannot be adjusted with the smallest silver pieces. For money, (made of Gold and silver) is to the τὰ χρήσα (that is to the matter of our Food and Covering) but as Farthings, and other local extrinsick money, is to the Gold and Silver species.

18. Now as the proportion of the number of Farthings requisite in comerse is to be taken from the number of people, the frequency of their exchanges; as also, and principally from the value of the smallest silver pieces of money; so in like maner, the proportion of money requisite to our Trade, is to be likewise taken from the frequency of commutations, and from the bigness of the payments, that are by Law or Custome usually made otherwise. From whence it follows, that where there are Registers of Lands, whereby the just

value of each mans interest in them, may be well known; and where there are Depositories of the τὰ χρὴςα, as of Metals, Cloth, Linnen, Leather, and other Usefuls; and where there are Banks of money also, there less money is necessary to drive the Trade. For if all the greatest payments be made in Lands, and the other perhaps down to ten pound, or twenty pound be made by credit in Lombars or Money-Banks: It follows, that there needs onely money to pay sums less then those aforementioned; just as fewer Farthings are requisite for change, where there be plenty of silver two Pences, then where the least silver piece is six Pence.

19. To apply all this, I say, that if there be too much money in a Nation, it were good for the Commonalty, as well as the King, and no harm even to particular men, if the King had in his Coffers, all that is superfluous, no more then if men were permitted to pay their Taxes in any thing they could best spare.

20. On the other side, if the largeness of a publick Exhibition should leave less money then is necessary to drive the Nations Trade, then the mischief thereof would be the doing of less work, which is the same as lessening the people, or their Art and Industry; for a hundred pound passing a hundred hands for Wages, causes a 10000*l.* worth of Commodities to be produced, which hands would have been idle and useless, had there not been this continual motive to their employment.

21. Taxes if they be presently expended upon our own Domestick Commodities, seem to me, to do little harm to the whole Body of the people, onely they work a change in the Riches and Fortunes of particular men; and particularly by transferring the same from the Landed and Lazy, to the Crafty and Industrious. As for example, if a Gentleman have let his Lands to Farm for a hundred pound *per annum*, for several years or lives, and he be taxed twenty pound *per annum*, to maintain a Navy; then the effect hereof will be, that this Gentleman's twenty pound *per annum*, will be distributed amongst Seamen, Ship-Carpenters, and other Trades relating to Naval matters; but if the Gentleman had his Land in his own hands, then being taxed a Fifth part, he would raise his Rents near the same proportion upon his under Tenants, or would sell his Cattle, Corn, and Wooll a Fifth part dearer; the like also would all other subdependents on him do; and thereby recover in some measure, what he paid. Lastly, but if all the money levied were thrown into the Sea, then the ultimate effect would onely be, that every man must work a fifth part the harder, or retrench a fifth part of his consumptions, *viz.* the former, if forreign Trade be improveable, and the latter, if it be not.

22. This, I conceive, were the worst of Taxes in a well policed State; but in other States, where is not a certain prevention of Beggary and Theevery, that is a sure livelihood for men wanting imployment; there, I confess, an

excessive Taxe, causes excessive and insuperable want, even of natural necessities, and that on a sudden, so as ignorant particular persons, cannot finde out what way to subsist by; and this, by the law of Nature, must cause sudden effects to relieve it self, that is, Rapines, Frauds; and this again must bring Death, Mutilations, and Imprisonments, according to the present Laws which are Mischiefs, and Punishments, as well unto the State, as to the particular sufferers of them.

CHAPTER. IV.

Of the several wayes of Taxe, and first, of setting a part, a proportion of the whole Territory for Publick uses, in the nature of Crown Lands; and secondly, by way of Assessement, or Land-taxe.

But supposing, that the several causes of Publick Charge are lessened as much as may be, and that the people be well satisfied, and contented to pay their just shares of what is needfull for their Government and Protection, as also for the Honour of their Prince and Countrey: It follows now to propose the several wayes, and expedients, how the same may be most easily, speedily, and insensibly collected. The which I shall do, by exposing the conveniencies and inconveniences of some of the principal wayes of Levyings, used of later years within the several States of *Europe*: unto which others of smaller and more rare use may be referred.

2. Imagine then, a number of people, planted in a Territory, who had upon Computation concluded, that two Millions of pounds *per annum*, is necessary to the publick charges. Or rather, who going more wisely to work, had computed a twenty fifth part of the proceed of all their Lands and Labours, were to be the *Excisum*, or the part to be cut out, and laid aside for publick uses. Which proportions perhaps are fit enough to the affairs of *England*, but of that hereafter.

3. Now the question is, how the one or the other shall be raised. The first way we propose, is, to Excize the very Land it self in kinde; that is, to cut out of the whole twenty five Millions, which are said to be in *England* and *Wales*, as much Land *in specie*, as whereof the Rack-rent would be two Millions, *viz.* about four Millions of Acres, which is about a sixth part of the whole; making the said four Millions to be Crown Lands, and as the four Counties intended to be reserved in *Ireland* upon the forfeitures were. Or else to excize a sixth part of the rent of the whole, which is about the proportion, that the Adventurers and Souldiers in *Ireland* retribute to the King, as Quit Rents. Of which two wayes, the latter is manifestly the better, the King having more security, and more obligees, provided the trouble and charge of this universal Collection, exceed not that of the other advantage considerably.

4. This way in a new State would be good, being agreed upon, as it was in *Ireland*, before men had even the possession of any Land at all; wherefore whosoever buyes Land in *Ireland* hereafter, is no more concerned with the Quit Rents wherewith they are charged, then if the Acres were so much the fewer; or then men are, who buy Land, out of which they know Tythes are to be paid. And truly that Countrey is happy, in which by Original Accord, such a Rent is reserved, as whereby the Publick charge may be born, without

contingent, sudden, superadditions, in which lies the very *Ratio* of the burthen of all Contributions and Exactions. For in such cases, as was said before, it is not onely the Landlord payes, but every man who eats but an Egg, or an Onion of the growth of his Lands; or who useth the help of any Artisan, which feedeth on the same.

5. But if the same were propounded in *England*, *viz.* if an aliquot part of every Landlords Rent were excinded or retrenched, then those whose Rents were settled, and determined for long times to come, would chiefly bear the burthen of such an Imposition, and others have a benefit thereby. For suppose A. and B. have each of them a parcel of Land, of equal goodness and value; suppose also that A. hath let his parcel for twenty one years at twenty pound *per annum*, but that B. is free; now there comes out a Taxe of a fifth part; hereupon B. will not let under 25*l.* that his remainder may be twenty, whereas A. must be contented with sixteen neat; nevertheless the Tenants of A. will sell the proceed of their bargain at the same rate, that the Tenants of B. shall do. The effect of all this is; First, that the Kings fifth part of B. his Farm, shall be greater then before. Secondly, that the Farmer to B. shall gain more then before the Taxe. Thirdly, that the Tenant or Farmer of A. shall gain as much as the King and Tenant to B. both. Fourthly, the Tax doth ultimately light upon the Landlord A. and the Consumptioners. From whence it follows, that a Land-taxe resolves into an irregular Excize upon consumptions, that those bear it most, who least complain. And lastly, that some Landlords may gain, and onely such whose Rents are predetermined shall loose; and that doubly, *viz.* one way by the raising of their revenues, and the other by enhansing the prices of provisions upon them.

6. Another way is an *Excisum* out of the Rent of Houseing, which is much more uncertain then that of Land. For an House is of a double nature, *viz.* one, wherein it is a way and means of expence; the other, as 'tis an Instrument and Tool of gain: for a Shop in *London* of less capacity and less charge in building then a fair Dining-Room in the same House, unto which both do belong, shall nevertheless be of the greater value; so also shall a Dungeon, Sellar, then a pleasant Chamber; because the one is expence, the other profit. Now the way of a Land-taxe rates housing, as of the latter nature, but the Excize, as of the former.

7. We might adde hereunto, that housing is sometimes disproportionally taxed to discourage Building, especially upon new Foundations, thereby to prevent the growth of a City; suppose *London*, such excessive and overgrown Cities being dangerous to Monarchy, though the more secure when the Supremacy is in Citizens of such places themselves, as in *Venice*.

8. But we say, that such checking of new Buildings signifies nothing to this purpose; for as much as Buildings do not encrease, until the People already

have increased: but the remedy of the abovementioned dangers is to be sought in the causes of the encrease of People, the which if they can be nipt, the other work will necessarily be done.

But what then is the true effect of forbidding to build upon new foundations? I answer to keep and fasten the City to its old seat and ground-plot, the which encouragement for new Buildings will remove, as it comes to pass almost in all great Cities, though insensibly, and not under many years progression.

9. The reason whereof is, because men are unwilling to build new houses at the charge of pulling down their old, where both the old house it self, and the ground it stands upon do make a much dearer ground-plot for a new house, and yet far less free and convenient; wherefore men build upon new free foundations, and cobble up old houses, until they become fundamentally irreparable, at which time they become either the dwelling of the Rascality, or in process of time return to waste and Gardens again, examples whereof are many even about *London*.

Now if great Cities are naturally apt to remove their Seats, I ask which way? I say, in the case of *London*, it must be Westward, because the Windes blowing near **3. 4.** of the year from the West, the dwellings of the West end are so much the more free from the fumes, steams, and stinks of the whole Easterly Pyle; which where Seacoal is burnt is a great matter. Now if it follow from hence, that the Pallaces of the greatest men will remove Westward, it will also naturally follow, that the dwellings of others who depend upon them will creep after them. This we see in *London*, where the Noblemens ancient houses are now become Halls for Companies, or turned Into Tenements, and All the Pallaces are Gotten Westward; Insomuch, As I Do Not Doubt but That Five Hundred Years Hence, The Kings Pallace will be near *Chelsey*, and the Old Building Of *Whitehall* converted to uses more answerable to their quality. For to build a new Royal Pallace upon the same ground will be too great a confinement, in respect of Gardens and other magnificencies, and withall a disaccommodation in the time of the work; but it rather seems to me, that the next Palace will be built from the whole present contignation of houses at such a distance as the old Pallace of *Westminster* was from the City of *London*, when the Archers began to bend their bowes just without *Ludgate*, and when all the space between the *Thames*, *Fleet-street*, and *Holborn* was as *Finsbury-Fields* are now.

10. This digression I confess to be both impertinent to the business of Taxes, and in it self almost needless; for why should we trouble our selves what shall be five hundred years hence, not knowing what a day may bring forth; and since 'tis not unlikely, but that before that time we may be all transplanted

from hence into *America*, these Countreys being overrun with Turks, and made waste, as the Seats of the famous Eastern Empires at this day are.

11. Onely I think 'tis certain, that while ever there are people in *England*, the greatest cohabitation of them will be about the place which is now *London*, the *Thames* being the most commodious River of this Island, and the seat of *London* the most commodious part of the *Thames*; so much doth the means of facilitating Carriage greaten a City, which may put us in minde of employing our idle hands about mending the High-wayes, making Bridges, Cawseys, and Rivers navigable: Which considerations brings me back round into my way of Taxes, from whence I digrest.

12. But before we talk too much of [Rents in order to Taxes, we]() should endeavour to explain the mysterious nature of them, with reference as well to Money, the rent of which we call usury; as to that of Lands and Houses, aforementioned.

13. Suppose a man could with his own hands plant a certain scope of Land with Corn, that is, could Digg, or Plough, Harrow, Weed, Reap, Carry home, Thresh, and Winnow so much as the Husbandry of this Land requires; and had withal Seed wherewith to sowe the same. I say, that when this man hath subducted his seed out of the proceed of his Harvest, and also, what himself hath both eaten and given to others in exchange for Clothes, and other Natural necessaries; that the remainder of Corn, is the natural and true Rent of the Land for that year; and the *medium* of seven years, or rather of so many years as makes up the Cycle, within which Dearths and Plenties make their revolution, doth give the ordinary Rent of the Land in Corn.

14. But a further, though collaterall question may be, how much English money this Corn or Rent is worth? I answer, so much as the money, which another single man can save, within the same time, over and above his expence, if he imployed himself wholly to produce and make it; *viz*. Let another man go travel into a Countrey where is Silver, there Dig it, Refine it, bring it to the same place where the other man planted his Corn; Coyne it, &c. the same person, all the while of his working for Silver, gathering also food for his necessary livelihood, and procuring himself covering, &c. I say, the Silver of the one, must be esteemed of equal value with the Corn of the other; the one being perhaps twenty Ounces, and the other twenty Bushels. From whence it follows, that the price of a Bushel of this Corn to be an Ounce of Silver.

15. And forasmuch as possibly there may be more Art and Hazzard in working about the Silver, then about the Corn, yet all comes to the same pass; for let a hundred men work ten years upon Corn, and the same number of men, the same time, upon Silver; I say, that the neat proceed of the Silver is the price of the whole neat proceed of the Corn, and like parts of the one,

the price of like parts of the other. Although not so many of those who wrought in Silver, learned the Art of refining and coining, or out-lived the dangers and diseases of working in the Mines. And this also is the way of pitching the true proportion, between the values of Gold and Silver, which many times is set but by popular errour, sometimes more, sometimes less, diffused in the world; which errour (by the way) is the cause of our having been pestred with too much Gold heretofore, and wanting it now.

16. This, I say, to be the foundation of equallizing and ballancing of values; yet in the superstructures and practices hereupon, I confess there is much variety, and intricacy; of which hereafter.

17. The world measures things by Gold and Silver, but principally the latter; for there may not be two measures, and consequently the better of many must be the onely of all; that is, by fine silver of a certain weight; but now if it be hard to measure the weight and fineness of silver, as by the different reports of the ablest Saymasters I have known it to be; and if silver granted to be of the same fineness and weight, rise and fall in its price, and be more worth at one place then another, not onely for being farther from the Mines, but for other accidents, and may be more worth at present, then a moneth or other small time hence; and if it differ in its proportion unto the several things valued by it, in several ages upon the increase and diminution thereof, we shall endeavour to examine some other natural Standards and Measures, without derogating from the excellent use of these.

18. Our Silver and Gold we call by severall names, as in *England* by pounds, shillings, and pence, all which may be called and understood by either of the three. But that which I would say upon this matter is, that all things ought to be valued by two natural Denominations, which is Land and Labour; that is, we ought to say, a Ship or garment is worth such a measure of Land, with such another measure of Labour; forasmuch as both Ships and Garments were the creatures of Lands and mens Labours thereupon: This being true, we should be glad to finde out a natural Par between Land and Labour, so as we might express the value by either of them alone as well or better then by both, and reduce one into the other as easily and certainly as we reduce pence into pounds. Wherefore we would be glad to finde the natural values of the Fee simple of Land, though but no better then we have done that of the *usus fructus* abovementioned, which we attempt as followeth.

19. Having found the Rent or value of the *usus fructus per annum*, the question is, how many years purchase (as we usually say) is the Fee simple naturally worth? If we say an infinite number, then an Acre of Land would be equal in value to a thousand Acres of the same Land; which is absurd, an infinity of unities being equal to an infinity of thousands. Wherefore we must pitch upon some limited number, and that I apprehend to be the number of years,

which I conceive one man of fifty years old, another of twenty eight, and another of seven years old, all being alive together may be thought to live; that is to say, of a Grandfather, Father, and Childe; few men having reason to take care of more remote Posterity: for if a man be a great Grandfather, he himself is so much the nearer his end, so as there are but three in a continual line of descent usually co-existing together; and as some are Grandfathers at forty years, yet as many are not till above sixty, and *sic de cæteris*.

20. Wherefore I pitch the number of years purchase, that any Land is naturally worth, to be the ordinary extent of three such persons their lives. Now in *England* we esteem three lives equal to one and twenty years, and consequently the value of Land, to be about the same number of years purchase. Possibly if they thought themselves mistaken in the one, (as the observator on the Bills of Mortality thinks they are) they would alter in the other, unless the confederation of the force of popular errour and dependance of things already concatenated, did hinder them.

21. This I esteem to be the number of years purchase where Titles are good, and where there is a moral certainty of enjoying the purchase. But in other Countreys Lands are worth nearer thirty years purchase, by reason of the better Titles, more people, and perhaps truer opinion of the value and duration of three lives.

22. And in some places, Lands are worth yet more years purchase by reason of some special honour, pleasures, priviledge or jurisdiction annexed unto them.

23. On the other hand, Lands are worth fewer years purchase (as in *Ireland*) for the following reasons, which I have here set down, as unto the like whereof the cause of the like cheapness in any other place may be imputed.

First, In *Ireland* by reason of the frequent Rebellions, (in which if you are conquered, all is lost; or if you conquer, yet you are subject to swarms of thieves and robbers) and the envy which precedent missions of English have against the subsequent, perpetuity it self is but forty years long, as within which time some ugly disturbance hath hitherto happened almost ever since the first coming of the English thither.

24. 2. The Claims upon Claims which each hath to the others Estates, and the facility of making good any pretence whatsoever by the favour of some one or other of the many Governours and Ministers which within forty years shall be in power there; as also by the frequency of false testimonies, and abuse of solemn Oaths.

25. 3. The paucity of Inhabitants, there being not above the **1. 5.** ^{th.} part so many as the Territory would maintain, and of those but a small part do work at all, and yet a smaller work so much as in other Countreys.

26. 4. That a great part of the Estates both real and personal in *Ireland* are owned by Absentees, and such as draw over the profits raised out of *Ireland* refunding nothing; so as *Ireland* exporting more then it imports doth yet grow poorer to a paradox.

27. 5. The difficulty of executing justice, so many of those in power being themselves protected by Offices, and protecting others. Moreover, the number of criminous and indebted persons being great, they favour their like in Juries, Offices, and wheresoever they can: Besides the Countrey is seldom rich enough to give due encouragement to profound Judges and Lawyers, which makes judgements very casual; ignorant men being more apt to be bold and arbitrary, then such as understand the dangers of it. But all this a little care in due season might remedy, so as to bring *Ireland* in a few years to the same level of values with other places; but of this also elsewhere more at large, for in the next place we shall come to Usury.

CHAPTER. V.

Of Usury.

What reason there is for taking or giving Interest or Usury for any thing which we may certainly have again whensoever we call for it, I see not; nor why Usury should be scrupled, where money or other necessaries valued by it, is lent to be paid at such a time and place as the Borrower chuseth, so as the Lender cannot have his money paid him back where and when himself pleaseth, I also see not. Wherefore when a man giveth out his money upon condition that he may not demand it back until a certain time to come, whatsoever his own necessities shall be in the mean time, he certainly may take a compensation for this inconvenience which he admits against himself: And this allowance is that we commonly call Usury.

2. And when one man furnisheth another with money at some distant place, and engages under great Penalties to pay him there, and at a certain day besides; the consideration for this, is that we call Exchange or local Usury.

As for example, if a man wanting money at *Carlisle* in the heat of the late Civil Wars, when the way was full of Souldiers and Robbers, and the passage by Sea very long, troublesome, and dangerous, and seldom passed; why might not another take much more then an 100*l.* at *London* for warranting the like summe to be paid at *Carlisle* on a certain day?

3. Now the Questions arising hence are; what are the natural Standards of Usury and Exchange? As for Usury, the least that can be, is the Rent of so much Land as the money lent will buy, where the security is undoubted; but where the security is casual, then a kinde of ensurance must be enterwoven with the simple natural Interest, which may advance the Usury very conscionably unto any height below the Principal it self. Now if things are so in *England*, that really there is no such security as abovementioned, but that all are more or less hazardous, troublesome, or chargeable to make, I see no reason for endeavoring to limit Usury upon time, any more then that upon place, which the practice of the world doth not, unless it be that those who make such Laws were rather Borrowers then Lenders: But of the vanity and fruitlessness of making Civil Positive Laws against the Laws of Nature, I have spoken elsewhere, and instanced in several particulars.

4. As for the natural measures of Exchange, I say, that in times of Peace, the greatest Exchange can be but the labour of carrying the money *in specie*, but where are hazards and emergent uses for money more in one place then another, &c. or opinions of these true or false, the Exchange will be governed by them.

5. Parallel unto this, is something which we omitted concerning the price of Land; for as great need of money heightens Exchange, so doth great need of Corn raise the price of that likewise, and consequently of the Rent of the Land that bears Corn, and lastly of the Land it self; as for example, if the Corn which feedeth *London*, or an Army, be brought forty miles thither, then the Corn growing within a mile of *London*, or the quarters of such Army, shall have added unto its natural price, so much as the charge of bringing it thirty nine miles doth amount unto: And unto perishable Commodities as fresh fish, fruits, &c. the ensurance upon the hazard of corrupting, &c. shall be added also; and finally unto him that eats these things there (suppose in Taverns) shall be added the charge of all the circumstancial apparatus of House-rent, Furniture, Attendance, and the Cooks skill as well as his labour to accompany the same.

6. Hence it comes to pass, that Lands intrinsically alike near populous places, such as where the perimeter of the Area that feeds them is great, will not onely yield more Rent for these Reasons, but also more years purchase then in remote places, by reason of the pleasure and honour extraordinary of having Lands there; for

———*Omne tulit punctum qui miscuit utile dulci.*

7. Having finished our digression upon the measures of the Rents and Values of Lands and Moneys, we now return to our second way of leavying Publick Charges, which was the taking of a proportion of the Rent, (commonly called Assessment) it follows next to speak of the way of computing the said Rents, otherwise then according to the bargains which a few men make one with another, through ignorance, haste, false suggestion, or else in their passion or drink: Although I acknowledge, that the medium or common result of all the bargains made within three years (or other such Cycle of time, as within which all contingencies of Land revolve) may be very sufficient to this purpose, being but the summe synthetically computed by casual opinions, as I would endeavour to cast up analytically by a distinct particularizing of the Causes.

8. 1. Therefore I propound a Survey of the Figures, Quantities, and Scituations of all the Lands both according to the civil bounds of Parishes, Farms, &c. and the natural distinctions thereof by the Sea, Rivers, ridges of Rocks, or Mountains, &c.

9. 2. I propound that the quality of each denomination were described by the Commodities it had usually born, in some Land, some sort of Timber, Grain, pulse or root growing more happily then in others: Also by the encrease of things sown or planted, which it hath yielded *communibus annis*; and withall,

the comparative goodness of the said Commodities not unto the common Standard money, but to one another. As for example; if there be ten acres of Land, I would have it judged whether they be better for Hay or Corn; if for Hay, whether the said ten Acres will bear more or less of Hay then ten other Acres; and whether an hundred weight of the said Hay will feed or fatten more or less, then the same weight of other Hay, and not as yet comparing it to money, in which the value of the said Hay will be more or less, according to the plenty of money, which hath changed strangely since the discovery of the *West Indies*, and according to the multitudes of people living near this Land, together with the luxurious or frugal living of them; and besides all, according to the Civil, Natural, and Religious Opinions of the said people: As for example, Eggs in the fore-part of Lent (because their goodness and delicacy decayes before Lent be done) being worth little in some Popish Countreys; nor Swines flesh among the Jews, nor Hedgehogs, Frogs, Snails, Mushrooms, &c. to those that fear to eat them, as poisonous or unwholesome; nor Currans and Spanish Wines, if they were all to be destroyed as the great thieves of this Nation, by an Edict of the State.

10. This former I call a Survey or Inquisition into the intrinsick Values of Land, this latter of extrinsick or accidentall follows. We said, that the change of the store of money would change the rates of commodities according to our reckoning in names and words, (pounds, shillings, and pence being nothing else) as for example:

If a man can bring to *London* an ounce of Silver out of the Earth in *Peru*, in the same time that he can produce a bushel of Corn, then one is the natural price of the other; now if by reason of new and more easie Mines a man can get two ounces of Silver as easily as formerly he did one, then Corn will be as cheap at ten shillings the bushel, as it was before at five shillings *cæteris paribus*.

11. It behoves us therefore to have a way, whereby to tell the money of our Countrey (which I think I have, and that in a short time, and without cost, and (which is more) without looking into particular mens pockets; of which hereafter.) Now if we know what Gold and Silver we had in *England* two hundred years ago, and could tell it again now; and though we also knew the difference of our denominations then, when thirty seven shillings were made out the same quantity of Silver as sixty two are now; also that of the alloy, labour in Coinage, remedies for weight and fineness, and duties to the King; nay, if we also knew the Labourers wages then and now, yet all this would not shew the difference of the Riches of our Nation even in money alone.

12. Wherefore we must adde to the premises, the knowledge of the difference of the numbers of the people, and conclude, that if all the money in the Nation were equally divided amongst all the people both then and now, that

that time wherein each Devisee had wherewith to hire most labourers, was the richer. So that we want the knowledge of the People and Bullion which is now in this Land, and which was heretofore; all which I think may be found out even for the time past, but more probably for the time present and to come.

13. But to proceed; suppose we had them, then we would pitch the accidental values upon our Lands about *London*; as thus, *viz.* We would first at hazzard compute the materials for food and covering, which the Shires of *Essex*, *Kent*, *Surrey*, *Middlesex* and *Hertford*, next circumjacent to *London*, did *communibus annis* produce; and would withal compute the Consumptioners of them living in the said five Shires and *London*. The which if I found to be more then were the Consumptioners living upon the like scope of other Land, or rather upon as much other Land as bore the like quantity of Provisions. Then I say, that Provisions must be dearer in the said five Shires then in the other; and within the said Shires cheaper or dearer as the way to *London* was more or less long, or rather more or less chargeable.

14. For if the said five Shires did already produce as much Commodity, as by all endeavour was possible; then what is wanting must be brought from a far, and that which is near, advanced in price accordingly; or if the said Shires by greater labour then now is used, (as by digging instead of Ploughing, setting instead of sowing, picking of choice seed instead of taking it promiscuously, steeping it instead of using it wholly unprepared, and manuring the ground with salt instead of rotten straw, &c. could be fertilized) then will the Rent be as much more advanced, as the excess of encrease exceeds that of the labour.

15. Now the price of labour must be certain, (as we see it made by the Statutes which limit the day wages of several workmen); the non-observance of which Laws, and the not adapting them to the change of times, is by the way very dangerous, and confusive to all endeavours of bettering the Trade of the Nation.

16. Moreover, the touchstone to try whether it be better to use those improvements or not, is to examine whether the labour of fetching these things even from the places where they grow wilde, or with less Culture, be not less then that of the said improvements.

17. Against all this will be objected, that these computations are very hard if not impossible to make; to which I answer onely this, that they are so, especially if none will trouble their hands or heads to make them, or give authority for so doing: But withall, I say, that until this be done, Trade will be too conjectural a work for any man to employ his thoughts about; for it will be the same wisdom in order to win with fair Dice, to spend much time in considering how to hold them, how much to shake them, and how hard

to throw them, and on what angles they should hit the side of the Tables, as to consider how to advance the Trade of this Nation; where at present particular men get from their neighbours (not from the earth and sea) rather by hit then wit, and by the false opinions of others, rather then their own judgements; Credit every where, but chiefly in *London*, being become a meer conceit, that a man is responsible or not, without any certain knowledge of his Wealth or true Estate. Whereas I think the nature of credit should be limited onely to an opinion of a mans faculties to get by his art and industry. The way of knowing his Estate being to be made certain, and the way of making him pay what he owes to the utmost of his ability, being to be expected from the good execution of our Laws.

18. I should here enlarge upon a Paradox, to prove that if every mans Estate could be always read in his forehead, our Trade would much be advanced thereby, although the poorer ambitious man be commonly the more industrious. But of this elsewhere.

19. The next objection against this so exact computation of the Rents and worth of Lands, &c. is, that the Sovereign would know too exactly every mans Estate; to which I answer, that if the Charge of the Nation be brought as low as it may be, (which depends much upon the people in Parliament to do) and if the people be willing and ready to pay, and if care be taken, that although they have not ready money, the credit of their Lands and Goods shall be as good; and lastly, that it would be a great discommodity to the Prince to take more then he needs, as was proved before; where is the evil of this so exact knowledge? And as for the proportion of every Contributor, why should any man hope or accept to ease himself by his craft and interest in a confusion? or why should he not fear, though he may be advantaged this time, to suffer in the next.

CHAPTER. VI.

Of Customs and Free Ports.

Custom is a Contribution or Excisum out of Goods sent out or imported into the Princes Dominions: In these Countreys of a twentieth part not according to the Prices currant among Merchants of each respective Commodity, but according to other standing Rates set by the State, though advised for the most part by concerned Persons.

2. I cannot well imagine what should be the natural Reasons, why a Prince should be paid this duty inward and outward both; there seems indeed to be some, why he should be paid for indulging the Exportation of some such things as other Countreys do really want.

3. Wherefore I think, that Customs at the first were a *præmium* allowed the Prince for protecting the Carriage of Goods both inward and outward from the Pyrats; and this I should verily believe, if the Prince were bound to make good losses of that kinde. And I thought that the proportion of five pound *per cent.* was pitched upon computation, that the Merchants before the said undertaking and composition, had usually lost more by Pyracy: And finally, that the Customs had been an ensurance upon losses by enemies, as the ensurance now usual, is of the casualties of sea, winde, weather and Vessel, or altogether; or like the ensurance in some Countreys of Houses from Fires for a certain small part of their yearly Rent. But be it what it will, it is anciently established by Law, and ought to be paid until it shall be abolished. Onely I take leave as an idle Philosopher to discourse upon the Nature and Measures of it.

4. The Measures of Customs outwards may be such, as after reasonable profit to the Exporter will leave such of our own Commodities as are necessary to Forreigners somewhat cheaper unto them then they can be had from elsewhere.

As for example, Tin is a Native Commodity, which governs the [Market abroad](), that is, there is none so good and so easie to be had and exported.

Now suppose Tin might be made in *Cornwall* for four pence the pound, and that the same would yield twelve pence at the nearest part in *France*, I say, that this extraordinary profit ought to be esteemed as a Mine Royal, or *Tresor Trové*, and the Sovereign ought to have his share in it: Which he will have, by imposing so great a duty upon Tin Exported, as on one side may leave a subsistence to the Workmen, (and no more) with a competent profit to the owners of the ground; and on the other side, may leave the price abroad less then that for which Tin may be had from any other place.

5. The same Imposition might also be made on the Tin spent at home, unless it be as impossible so to do, as for the King of *France* to impose the Gabel upon Salt in the very places where it is made.

6. But it is observed, that such high duties make men endeavour not to enter any such Goods at all, or pay for them, provided the charge of smuckling and bribing, with the hazzard of being seized do not *communibus vicibus* exceed the Duty.

7. Wherefore the Measures of this Nature are, that it be more easie, safe, and profitable for men to keep the Law, then to break it, unless it be in such cases, where the Magistrate can with certainty execute the Law. As for example, it would be hard to save the Duties upon Horses shipped at a small Port, without adjacent Creeks, and that but some certain two hours every Tide, forasmuch as Horses cannot be disguised, put up in bags or cask, nor shipped without noise and the help of many hands.

8. The Measures of Customs upon imported Commodities are; 1. That all things ready and ripe for Consumption may be made somewhat dearer then the same things grown or made at home; if the same be feasible *cæteris paribus*.

2. That all Superfluities tending to Luxury and sin, might be loaded with so much Impost, as to serve instead of a sumptuary Law to restrain the use of them. But here also care is to be had that it be not better to smuckle then to pay.

9. On the contrary, all things not fully wrought and Manufactured, as raw Hides, Wool, Beaver, Raw-silk, Cotton; as also all Tools and Materials for Manufacture, as also Dying-stuff, &c. ought to be gently dealt with.

10. If to leavy the payment of these Duties could be most exactly performed, Princes might strangely practice one upon another; wherefore since they cannot, the people pay no more then they cannot with greater safety upon the whole matter save, nor observe any more of these Laws, then they cannot elude.

11. The Inconveniences of the way of Customs, are, *viz*.

1. That Duties are laid upon things not yet ripe for use, upon Commodities in *fieri*, and but in the way of their full improvements, which seems the same ill-husbandry, as to make fuel of young Saplings, instead of Dotards and Pollards.

2. The great number of Officers requisite to Collect the said Duties, especially in a Countrey where the Harbours are many, and the Tides convenient for shipping of Goods at any time.

3. The great facility of smuckling by Briberies, Collusions, hiding and disguising of Commodities, &c. and all this notwithstanding Oaths and Penalties, and withall by the several wayes of mitigating and taking off the said Penalties even after discovery.

4. The Customs or Duties upon the few Commodities of the growth of *England* exchanged with Foreigners, make too small a part of the whole Expence of the people of this Kingdom, which (perhaps is not less then fifty millions of pounds *per annum*) out of which to bear the common Charges thereof, so as some other way of Leavy must be practised together with it; whereas by some one way, if the best, the whole work may be absolved: wherefore 'tis an inconvenience in the way of Customs, that it necessitates other wayes then it self.

12. Now as a small attempt of a Remedy or Expedient herein, I offer rather, that instead of the Customs upon Goods shipped, every Ship that goes in or out, may pay a Tonnage, the same being collectible by a very few hands, as a matter visible to all the world; and that the said Duty be but such a part of the Fraight, as the like whereof being excinded out of the whole Consumption, would defray all the Publique Charge; which part perhaps is 4. *per Cent.* or thereabouts, *viz.* two millions *per annum* out of fifty.

13. The other is, that the Customs be reduced into the nature of an Ensurance-*præmium*, and that the same be augmented and fitted, as whereby the King may afford to ensure the goods as well against the Sea as Enemies; by which means the whole Nation would be concerned in all such losses, and then the Merchant for his own sake would more willingly enter and pay for whatsoever he would have ensured.

14. But it will be here objected, that although the duty of Customs be abrogated, yet that there must be almost the same number of Officers maintained as now to prevent the bringing in and carrying out of prohibited Commodities. Wherefore we shall here state the nature of such Prohibitions by two or three grand instances.

15. To prohibit the Exportation of Money, in that it is a thing almost impracticable, it is almost nugatory and vain; And the danger of it resolves either into a kinde of Ensurance answerable to the danger of being seized, or unto a Surcharge of a Composition by bribing the Searchers. As for example, If but one in fifty Exportations are seized, or if twenty shillings be usually taken for conniving at fifty pounds, then the Commodities bought with this Money must be sold two at least *per cent.* the dearer to the Consumptioner. Now if the Trade will not bear this Surcharge, then Money will not be exported with discretion. Now the use of this Prohibition, supposing it practicable, is to serve as a sumptuary Law, and to binde the Nation in general not to spend more then they get; for if we could export no Commodity of

our own growth or manufacture then by prohibiting the going out of Money, it is also *ipso facto* commanded that nothing forreign should be brought in. Again supposing, that ordinarily we export enough to furnish us with all Forreign Commodities, but upon some extraordinary decay of our Land or hands, we are able to export but half as much as would procure our ordinary proportion of Forreign Goods, then the Prohibition of Money performs indeed the part of a sumptuary Law, in hindring us to bring in any more then half as much Forreign Commodities as we formerly used, onely it leaves it to the discretion of the Merchant, to chose which he will neglect or forbear to bring in, and which not; whereas in sumptuary Laws the State taketh this care upon themselves. As for example, If we wanted Exportation to ballance our Importations by forty thousand pounds, and suppose for examples sake, that the Importation of forty thousand pounds worth of Coffee-Berries, or the like of Spanish Wine must be retrenched; in this case, the said Prohibition of Money will do one, or some of the one, and some of the other as the Merchant himself pleases: But the sumptuary Law determines, whether we shall encourage and keep fair with the Nation that sends us Wine rather then that which sends us Coffee, and whether the Expence of Wine or Coffee be most prejudicial to our people, &c.

16. The benefits alledged for the free Exportation of Money is meerly this, *viz*. That if a Ship carrying out of *England* forty thousand pounds worth of Cloth, might also carry with it forty thousand pounds in Money, then could the Merchant stand the stiffer upon his terms, and in fine would buy cheaper, and sell dearer; but by the way, the Merchant buyes this power with the Interest and advantage of the Money he carries, which if it amount to five pound *per Cent*. then he had better sold his Goods at four pound *per Cent*. under rate, then to have fortified himself with Money as aforesaid. But of this more may be said, we hasten to the great point of Wool.

17. The Hollanders having gotten away our Manufacture of Cloth, by becoming able to work with more art, to labour and fare harder, to take less fraight, Duties and Ensurance, hath so madded us here in *England*, that we have been apt to think of such exorbitantly fierce wayes of prohibiting Wool and Earth to be exported, as perhaps would do us twice as much harm as the losse of our said Trade. Wherefore to return to our Wits and Trade again, before we can tell what to do in this case, we must consider;

1. That we are often forced to buy Corn from abroad, and as often complain that we are pestered with abundance of idle hands at home, and withall that we cannot vend the Woollen Manufactures even which our few working hands do produce. In this case were it not better to lessen our sheep-trade, and convert our hands to more Tillage? Because 1. Flesh becomming dearer,

there would be encouragement for Fish, which will never be till then. 2. Our Money would not run so fast away for Corn. 3. We should have no such Gluts of Wool upon our hands. 4. Our idle hands would be employed in Tillage and Fishing, one man by the way of grazing, tilling as it were many thousand Acres of Land by himself and his Dog.

2. Suppose we wanted no Corn, nor had any idle hands, and yet that we abounded with more Wool then we can work up; in this case certainly Wool might be exported, because 'tis supposed, that the hands which work are already employed upon a better Trade.

3. Suppose the Hollander outdo us by more art, were it not better to draw over a number of their choice Workmen, or send our most ingenious men thither to learn; which if they succeed; it is most manifest, that this were the more natural way, then to keep that infinite clutter about resisting of Nature, stopping up the windes and seas, &c.

4. If we can make Victual much cheaper here then in *Holland*, take away burdensome, frivolous, and antiquated Impositions and Offices.

I conceive even this were better then to perswade Water to rise of it self above its natural Spring.

5. We must consider in general, that as wiser Physicians tamper not excessively with their Patients, rather observing and complying with the motions of nature, then contradicting it with vehement Administrations of their own; so in Politicks and Oconomicks the same must be used; for

Naturam expellas furcâ licet usque recurrit.

18. Nevertheless, if the Hollanders advantages in making Cloth be but small and few in comparison of ours, that is, if they have but a little the better of us, then I conceive that Prohibitions to export Wool may sufficiently turn the scales. But whether this be so or not, I leave to others, being my self neither Merchant nor Statesman.

19. As for Prohibition of Importations, I say that it needs not be, until they much exceed our Exportations. For if we should think it hard to give good necessary Cloth for debauching Wines, yet if we cannot dispose of our Cloth to others, 'twere better to give it for Wine or worse, then to cease making it; nay, better to burn a thousand mens labours for a time, then to let those thousand men by non-employment lose their faculty of labouring. In brief, what may be further said hereupon, resolves into the Doctrine and *Ingenium* of making sumptuary Laws, and judicious use of them *pro hic & nunc*.

20. Unto this Discourse of Customs appertains that of Free Ports, which (in a Nation that onely trades for it self, *viz.* vents its own superfluities, and imports onely Necessaries for it self) are of no use, but rather harm; for

suppose Wines be brought into a Free Port, be there housed and privately sold, but the Cask filled up with stained water, and put on ship-board again to be staved as soon as the ship is out at sea: In this case, the Duties of those Wines are defrauded, as it also may be many other wayes.

21. Now if it be said, that although we should trade but for our selves, yet that our Ports (being more commodious then those of other Nations) would be the more frequented; for being free, and consequently the more enriched, by the expence of Sea-men and Passengers, hire of Labourers, and Warehouses, &c. even without any Custom at all upon the Goods. Nevertheless 'tis reason that a small duty should be paid upon the ship as aforesaid for such use of our Ports, and that *eo nomine*; not expecting all our Benefit from the said hire of Cellaridge, Porters, and Carmen, which also might be had over and above for their proper reasons.

22. But if we could attain to be the Merchants between other Nations, there is then no reason for exacting Duties (as was said before) upon things *in fieri*, and which are but in the way of their improvement: And as for the fraud that may be committed, as in the case of Wines abovementioned, I affirm that our Excize upon the Consumption, would overcome and elude them.

CHAPTER. VII.

Of Poll-money.

Poll-money is a Tax upon the Persons of men, either upon all simply and indifferently, or else according to some known Title or mark of distinction upon each; and that either of bare honour, or else of some Office sought or imposed, or of some Faculty and Calling without respect to Riches or Poverty, Incomes or Expence, Gain or Loss accrewing by the said Title, Office, or Faculty.

2. The Poll-moneys which have been leavied of late have been wonderfully confused; as taxing some rich single persons at the lowest rate; some Knights, though wanting necessaries, at twenty pounds, encouraging some vain fellows to pay as Esquires, on purpose to have themselves written Esquires in the Receipts; making some pay ten pounds as Doctours of Physick or Law, who get nothing by the Faculty, nor minde the practice; making some poor Tradesmen forced to be of the Liveries of their Companies to pay beyond their strength; and lastly, some to pay according to their Estates, the same to be valued by those that know them not; thereby also giving opportunity to some Bankrupts to make the world credit them as men of such Estates, at which the Assessors did rate them by Collusion.

3. So as by this Confusion, Arbitraries, Irregularities, and hotch-pot of Qualifications, no estimate could be made of the fitness of this Plaister to the Sore, nor no Checque or way to examine whether the respective Receipts were duly accompted for, &c.

4. Wherefore wholly rejecting the said complicated way of Tax, I shall speak of Poll-money more distinctly, and first of the simple Poll-money upon every head of all mankinde alike; the Parish paying for those that receive alms, Parents for their Children under age, and Masters for their Apprentices, and others who receive no wages.

5. The evil of this way is, that it is very unequal; men of unequal abilities, all paying alike, and those who have greatest charges of Children paying most; that is, that by how much the poorer they are, by so much the harder are they taxed.

6. The Conveniencies are; first, that it may be suddenly collected, and with small charge: Secondly, that the number of the people being alwayes known, it may be sufficiently computed what the same will amount unto. Thirdly, It seems to be a spur unto all men, to set their Children to some profitable employment upon their very first capacity, out of the proceed whereof, to pay each childe his own Poll-money.

7. The next Poll-money is upon every head, but distinguished by Titles of meer Honour, without any kinde of Office or Faculty; as, Dukes, Marquesses, Earls, Viscounts, Barons, Baronets, Knights, and Esquires, *viz.* the eldest Sons of Knights *in perpetuum*, and Gentlemen if they write themselves so. This way is much more equal then the other; forasmuch as those who are Titled, are for the most part rich proportionably; or if they were not, yet men so dignified shall command a preheminence and place, even although they do not or cannot buy it of the vulgar by their Expence: my meaning hereby is, that a Title may possibly save a man as much as his Poll-money, may exceed the Plebeian Level by reason of such title.

8. Moreover, good and multiform Accompts being kept of the People, this Tax may be also easily speedily and inexpensively collected; and also being capable of being computed aforehand, may be fitted and seized according to the needs of the Prince.

9. As for Offices, they are indeed Dignities for the most part, but paid for by the trouble of administring them; as for example, to be an Alderman suppose of *London*, is indeed an honour, yet many pay five hundred pounds to be excused from receiving it.

Nevertheless it may not be improper to tax Offices sought; or such as are accepted although they might be refused: And on the other side no *Titulado* should be forced to pay Poll-money according to his Title, if he be contented to lay it down, and never resume it more.

10. The Titles of Faculties and Callings ought to be no Qualification in a Poll-money, because they do not necessarily nor probably inferr ability to pay, but carry with them vaste inequalities. But therefore if a man by his Licence to practise get much, it may be presumed he will spend accordingly; in which net the way of Excize will certainly take him, as it will all the Officers aforementioned.

11. Harth-money seems to be a Poll-money, but is not, being rather a way of Accumulative Excize; of which hereafter.

CHAPTER. VIII.

Of Lotteries.

Men that accept Titles may foresee, that they may be taxed by them as aforesaid, (although it be unlikely (one House of Parliament being all Tituladoes, and the greatest part of the other being such also) that any such way of Leavy should pass) and therefore they do as it were *à priori* consent unto the Tax in their own Individuals.

2. Now in the way of Lottery men do also tax themselves in the general, though out of hopes of Advantage in particular: A Lottery therefore is properly a Tax upon unfortunate self-conceited fools; men that have good opinion of their own luckiness, or that have believed some Fortune-teller or Astrologer, who had promised them great success about the time and place of the Lottery, lying Southwest perhaps from the place where the destiny was read.

3. Now because the world abounds with this kinde of fools, it is not fit that every man that will, may cheat every man that would be cheated; but it is rather ordained, that the Sovereign should have the Guardianship of these fools, or that some Favourite should beg the Sovereigns right of taking advantage of such mens folly, even as in the case of Lunaticks and Idiots.

4. Wherefore a Lottery is not tollerated without authority, assigning the proportion in which the people shall pay for their errours, and taking care that they be not so much and so often couzened, as they themselves would be.

5. This way of Lottery is used but for small Leavies, and rather upon privato-publick accompts, (then for maintaining Armies or Equipping Fleets,) such as are Aque-Ducts, Bridges, and perhaps Highwayes, &c. Wherefore we shall say no more of it upon this occasion.

CHAPTER. IX.

Of Benevolence.

The raising of Money by Benevolence, seems to be no force upon any man, nor to take from any man but what himself knows he can spare, nevertheless there is more in it; for to be but brow-beaten by a Prince or Grandee, proves often as heavy as to be distrained upon for an Assessment or Subsidy; and the danger of being misrepresented by linsy Pick-thanks and Informers as disaffected to the Cause for which the Leavy is made, is more frequent then the payment of any summe in a due proportion with all other men (which I have said is no impoverishment) can possibly be hurtful.

The benefits of this way are these, *viz.* That forasmuch as it sometimes falls out (as in the late Differences with the Scots, *annis* 1638. and 1639. when the Church Dignitaries were most concerned) that the cause of the Expence concerns some men more then others, that then an Imposition should not pass upon all for the sakes of a part: Sometimes it happens, that one sort of men have received greater and fresher favours then another; as upon the late Restoration of his Majesty *Anno* 1660. those who needed an Act of Indempnity did: And sometimes it is visible, that some men have had better times of gain and advantages then others, as the Clergy most eminently have had since his Majesties said Restoration. In all these Cases, the proposal of a Benevolence may be offered, although in no cases it be without its inconveniencies; the which are principally these.

1. The abovementioned Brow-beating and distaste given, if a man have not contributed as largely as envious observers think he should have done.

2. A Benevolence in many cases may divide a whole Nation into parties, or at least make the strength of Parties too well known to such as need not know it: and withall it may (on the contrary and upon design) disguize the same, and elude the measures which the Governours thought to have taken by such an exploratory artifice.

3. Some men may have particular reasons to contribute large, *viz.* complacency with, and hopes of being repaired by the favour of some Grandee, who favours the business, and the very same may make to the prejudice of others.

4. Men of sinking Estates, (who nevertheless love to live high, and appear splendid, and such who make themselves friends, (by their hospitality paid for, in effect by others) enough to be protected, even from Justice) do often upon this occasion of Benevolence set extravagant Examples unto others, who have laboured hardly for what they have; those not caring what they

pay, because it encreaseth their credit, to borrow the more, so as at length the whole burthen of such Bankrupts Benevolence, lights upon the frugal Patriots, by whom the Publique Weal subsists.

CHAPTER. X.

Of Penalties.

The usual Penalties are Death, Mutilations, Imprisonment, Publick disgrace, Corporal transient pains, and great Tortures, besides Pecuniary Mulcts. On which last we shall most insist, speaking of the others but in order to examine whether they may not be commuted for these.

2. There be some certain Crimes, for which the Law of God appoints death; and these must be punished with it, unless we say that those were but the Civil Laws of the Jewish Commonwealth, although given by God himself; of which opinion certainly most modern States are, in as much as they punish not Adulteries, &c. with death, as among the Jewes, and yet punish small Thefts with Death instead of multiple reparation.

3. Upon this supposition we shall venture to offer; whether the reason of simple Death be not to punish incorrigible Committers of great faults?

4. Of publick Death with Torments, to affright men from Treasons, which cause the deaths and miseries of many thousand innocent and useful people?

5. Of Death secretly executed, to punish secret and unknown Crimes, such as Publick Executions would teach to the World? Or else to suffocate betimes some dangerous Novelties in Religion, which the patient suffering of the worst man would much spread and encourage.

6. Mutilations suppose of Ears, Nose, &c. are used for perpetual disgrace, as standing in the Pillory is for temporary and transient; which and such other punishments have (by the way) made some corrigible offenders, to become desperate and incurable.

7. Mutilations of parts as of Fingers, are proper to disable such as have abused their dextrous use of them, by Pocket-picking, Counterfeiting of Seals and Writings, &c. Mutilations of other parts, may serve to punish and prevent Adulteries, Rapes, Incests, &c. And the smaller Corporal pains, serve to punish those, who can pay no pecuniary mulcts.

8. Imprisonment seems rather to be the punishments of suspected then guilty persons, and such as by their carriage give the Magistrate occasion to think, either they have done some smaller particular Crime, as Thefts, &c. or that they would commit greater, as Treasons and Seditions. But where Imprisonment is not a securing men untill their Trialls, but a sentence after Triall, it seems to me proper onely to seclude such men from conversation, whose Discourses are bewitching, and Practices infectious, and in whom

neverthelesse remains some hopes of their future Amendments, or usefulnesse for some service not yet appearing.

9. As for perpetual Imprisonment by sentence, it seems but the same with death it self, to be executed by nature it self, quickened with such Diseases, as close living, sadness, solitude, and reflections upon a past and better condition, doth commonly beget: Nor do men sentenced hereunto live longer, though they be longer in dying.

10. Here we are to remember in consequence of our opinion, [That Labour is the Father and active principle of Wealth, as Lands are the Mother] that the State by killing, mutilating, or imprisoning their members, do withall punish themselves; wherefore such punishments ought (as much as possible) to be avoided and commuted for pecuniary mulcts, which will encrease labour and publick wealth.

11. Upon which account, why should not a man of Estate, found guilty of man-slaughter, rather pay a certain proportion of his whole Estate, then be burnt in the hand?

12. Why should not insolvent Thieves be rather punished with slavery then death? so as being slaves they may be forced to as much labour, and as cheap fare, as nature will endure, and thereby become as two men added to the Commonwealth, and not as one taken away from it; for if *England* be under-peopled, (suppose by half) I say that next to the bringing in of as many more as now are, is the making these that are, to do double the work which now they do; that is, to make some slaves; but of this elsewhere.

13. And why should not the solvent Thieves and Cheats be rather punished with multiple Restitutions then Death, Pillory, Whipping? &c. But it will be asked, with how manifold Restitutions should picking a pocket (for example) be punished? I say, 'twere good in order to the solution hereof, to enquire of some candid Artists in that Trade, how often they are taken one time with another practising in this work? If but once in ten times, then to restore even but seven-fold, would be a fair profit; and to restore but ten-fold, were but an even lay; wherefore to restore twenty-fold, that is, double to the hazard, is rather the true *ratio* and measure of punishment by double reparation.

14. And surely the restoring two, three, four, and seven-fold mentioned in *Moses* Law must be thus understood, or else a man might make thieving a very fair and lawful profession.

15. The next question is, in such multiple Restitutions how many parts should be given to the sufferer. To which I answer, never above one, and scarce

that, to oblige him to more care, and self-preservation, with three parts to discoverers, and the rest to publick uses.

16. Thirdly, In the case of Fornications, most of the punishments not made by pecuniary mulcts and commuted, are but shame, and that too but towards some few persons, which shame for ever after obdurates the Offender, what ever it work upon such whose fames are yet intire: Of all which men take little consideration, standing upon the brink of such precipices as makes them giddy; and when they are in danger of such faults as are rather madnesses, distempers, and alienations of the minde and reason, as also insurrections of the passions, then deliberate acts of the understanding.

17. Moreover, according to that Axiom of *In quo quis peccat, in eodem puniatur*; if the *Ratio formalis* of the sin of *Concubitus Vagi*, be the hindering of procreation, let those who by their miscarriages of this kinde are guilty thereof, repair unto the State the misse of another pair of hands with the double labour of their own, or which is all one, by a pecuniary mulct; and this is the practice of some wise States in punishing what they will never be able to prevent: Nor doth the Gospel specifie any punishment in this world, onely declaring they shall not be received into the joyes of the next.

18. I could instance in more particulars, but if what I have already said be reasonable, this little is enough; if not, then all the rest would be too little also: wherefore I shall adde but one instance more, as most suitable to our present times and occasions, which is the way of punishing Heterodox Professors of Religion.

19. That the Magistrate may punish false Believers, if he believe he shall offend God in forbearing it, is true; for the same reasons that men give for Liberty of Conscience, and universal tolleration; and on the other side, that he may permit false Worships, seems clearly at least by the practice of all States, who allow Ambassadours their freedom (be their Worship never so abominable) even when they come to negociate but upon temporal and small matters.

20. Wherefore, since the Magistrate may allow or connive at such Worships as himself thinks fit, and yet may also punish; and since by Death, Mutilations, and imprisonments of the Subjects, the State not onely punisheth it self, but spreadeth the Pseudodoxies; it follows, that pecuniary Mulcts are the fittest wayes of checking the wantonness of men in this particular: forasmuch as that course favours of no bitterness at all, but rather argues a desire to indulge, provided such indulgence may consist with the indempnity of the State; for no Heterodox believer will desire to be tollerated longer then he keeps the Publick Peace; the which if he means to do, he cannot take it ill of the Magistrate, to keep him steddy unto that his duty, nor

grudge to contribute towards so much charge for that purpose as himself occasions.

21. Moreover, as there seems a reason for indulging some conscientious misbelievers, so there is as much for being severe towards Hypocrites, especially such as abuse holy Religion to cloak and vizzard worldly ends: Now what more easie and yet effectual way is there to discern between these two, then well proportioned pecuniary mulcts? for who desiring to serve God without fear, and labouring ten hours *per diem* at his Calling, would not labour one hour more for such a freedom? even as religious men spend an hour *per diem* more then the looser sort do at their Devotions; or who wearing Cloth of one and twenty shillings the yard, would not be contented with that of twenty shillings, for the same advantage of his liberty in Worship? Those that kick at this, being unwilling either to do or suffer for God, for whose sake they pretend so much.

22. It may be here objected, that although some bad Religions might be tollerated, yet that all may not, *viz.* such as consist not with the Civil Peace. To which I answer,

First; that there is no Schisme or Separation be it never so small, consistent with that unity and peace as could be wisht; nor none so perfectly conscientious, but may also be civilly most pernicious: For that *Venner* and his Complices acted upon internal motives, the most free exposing of themselves to death may evince; and yet their holding the King to be an Usurper upon the Throne and Right of Jesus Christ was a Civil mischief neither to be pardoned or parallel'd.

23. And yet on the other hand there is no Pseudodoxy so great, but may be muzzled from doing much harm in the State, without either Death, Imprisonment, or Mutilation: To make short, no opinion can be more dangerous, then to disbelieve the immortality of the Soul, as rendring man a beast, and without conscience, or fear of committing any evil, if he can but elude the penalties of humane Laws made against it, and letting men loose to all evil thoughts and designs whereof man can take no notice: Now I say, that even this Misbeliever may be adæquately punished if he be kept as a beast, be proprietor of nothing, as making no conscience how he gets; be never admitted in Evidence or Testimony, as under no Obligation to speak truth; be excluded all Honours and Offices, as caring onely for himself, not the protecting of others; and be withall kept to extream bodily labour, the profit whereof to the State is the pecuniary Mulct we speak of, though the greatest.

24. As for opinions less horrible then this, the Mulct may be fitted to each of them respectively, according to the measure of danger which the Magistrate apprehends from their allowance, and the charge necessary to prevent it.

25. And now we are speaking of the wayes how to prevent and correct Heterodoxies in Religion, which we have hitherto done by designing punishments for the erring sheep, I think it not amiss to adde, That in all these cases the Shepherds themselves should not wholly scape free: For if in this Nation there be such abundance of Free-Schools, and of liberall Maintenance provided in our Universities and elsewhere for instructing more then enough in all such learning as is fit to defend the established Religion, together with superabundant Libraries for that purpose. Moreover, if the Church-preferments be so numerous and ample both for Wealth, Honour, and Power, as scarce any where more; it seems strange that when by the laziness, formality, ignorance, and loose lives of our Pastours, the sheep have gone astray, grown scabbed, or have been devoured by Wolves and Foxes, that the Remedy of all this should be onely sought by frighting those that have strayed from ever returning again, and by tearing off as well the skins as the wool of those that are scabbed; whereas Almighty God will rather require the blood even of them that have been devoured, from the shepheards themselves.

26. Wherefore if the Minister should lose part of the Tythes of those whom he suffers to defect from the Church, (the defector not saving, but the State wholly gaining them) and the defector paying some pecuniary Mulct for his Schisme, and withall himself defraying the charge of his new particular Church and Pastorage, me thinks the burthen would be thus more equally born.

27. Besides, the judicious world do not believe our Clergy can deserve the vaste preferments they have, onely because they preach, give a better accompt of Opinions concerning Religion then others, or can express their conceptions in the words of the Fathers, or the Scriptures, &c. Whereas certainly the great honour we give them, is for being patterns of holiness, for shewing by their own self-denials, mortifications, and austerities, that 'tis possible for us to imitate them in the precepts of God; for if it were but for their bare Pulpit-discourses, some men might think there is ten thousand times as much already printed as can be necessary, and as good as any that ever hereafter may be expected. And it is much suspected, that the Discipline of the Cloisters hath kept up the Roman Religion, which the Luxury of the Cardinals and Prelates might have destroyed.

28. The substance therefore of all we have said in this discourse concerning the Church is, that it would make much for its peace, if the Nursery of Ministers be not too big, that Austerities in the Priests lives would reconcile

them to the people; and that it is not unreasonable, that when the whole Church suffers by the defection of her Members, that the Pastours of it by bearing a small part should be made sensible of the loss; the manner and measures of all which I leave unto those unto whom it belongs.

29. Concerning Penalties and Penal Laws I shall adde but this, that the abuse of them is, when they are made not to keep men from sin, but to draw them into punishment; and when the Executers of them keep them hid until a fault be done, and then shew them terrible to the poor immalicious offender: Just like Centinels, who never shew men the advertisements against pissing near their Guards, till they have catcht them by the coats for the forfeiture they claim.

CHAPTER. XI.

Of Monopolies and Offices.

Monopoly (as the word signifies) is the sole selling power, which whosoever hath can vend the commodity whereupon he hath this power, either qualified as himself pleases, or at what price he pleaseth, or both, within the limits of his Commission.

2. The great example of a Monopoly is the King of *France* his Gabel upon Salt, whereby he sells that for sixty which costs him but one; now Salt being a thing of universal use to all degrees of men, and scarce more to the poor then the rich, it seems to be of the same effect with the simplest Poll-money abovementioned, in case all men spent equally of it, or if men be forced to take it whether they spend it or not, as in some places they are. But if men spend or eat Salt unequally, as they commonly do, nor are bound to take or pay for more then they spend, then it is no other then an accumulative Excize, especially if the salt be all of one uniform goodness, otherwise it is a distinct species of Leavy, *viz.* a Monopoly.

3. The use or pretence of instituting a Monopoly is,

First, Right of Invention; forasmuch as the Laws do reward Inventions, by granting them a Monopoly of them for a certain time; (as here in *England* for fourteen years) for thereby the Inventor is rewarded more or less according to the acceptance which his Invention findes amongst men.

Where note by the way, that few new Inventions were ever rewarded by a Monopoly; for although the Inventor often-times drunk with the opinion of his own merit, thinks all the world will invade and incroach upon him, yet I have observed, that the generality of men will scarce be hired to make use of new practices, which themselves have not thoroughly tried, and which length of time hath not vindicated from latent inconveniences; so as when a new Invention is first propounded, in the beginning every man objects, and the poor Inventor runs the Gantloop of all petulent wits; every man finding his several flaw, no man approving it, unless mended according to his own advice: Now not one of an hundred out-lives this torture, and those that do, are at length so changed by the various contrivances of others, that not any one man can pretend to the Invention of the whole, nor well agree about their respective shares in the parts. And moreover, this commonly is so long a doing, that the poor Inventor is either dead, or disabled by the debts contracted to pursue his design; and withall railed upon as a Projector, or worse, by those who joyned their money in partnership with his wit; so as the said Inventor and his pretences are wholly lost and vanisht.

Secondly, a Monopoly may be of real use for a time, *viz.* at the first introducing of a new Manufacture, wherein is much nicety to make it well, and which the generality of men cannot judge of as to the performance. As for example; suppose there were some most approved Medicament which one certain man could make most exactly well, although several others could also make the same less perfectly: in this case this same chief Artist may be allowed a Monopoly for a time, *viz.* until others have had experience enough under him, how to make the Medicament as well as himself. First, because the world may not have the Medicament variously made, when as they can neither discern the difference by their senses, nor judge of the effects thereof *à posteriori*, by their reasons. Secondly, because others may be fully instructed by him that can best do it; and thirdly, because he may have a reward for such his communications: But forasmuch as by Monopolies of this kinde, great Leavies are seldom made, they are scarce pertinent to our design.

Offices instituted by the State with Fees of their own appointment, are of parallel nature to Monopolies; the one relating to actions and employments as the other to things, and have the same to be said for and against them as Monopolies have.

As a Kingdom encreaseth and flourisheth, so doth variety of things, of actions, and even of words encrease also; for we see that the language of the most flourishing Empires was ever the most copious and elegant, and that of mountainous Cantons the contrary: Now as the actions of this Kingdom encreased, so did the Offices (that is, the power and faculty of solely executing and performing the said actions) encrease likewise; and on the contrary, as the business of Offices encreased, so did the difficulty and danger of discharging them amiss decrease proportionably: from whence 'tis come to pass, that the Offices which at their first erecting were not performed but by the ablest, most inventive, and versatile Instruments, (such as could wrestle with all emergent difficulties, and collect Rules and Axioms out of the Series of their own Observations, (with reference to the various casualties of their employments) whereby to direct Posterity) are now performed by the most ordinary, formal, pack-horse Deputies and Sub-Deputies.

And whereas at first such large Fees were allowed as (considering even the paucity of them which might then be received) should compensate the Art, Trust, and Industry of the Administratour; yet the said large Fees are still continued, although the skill and trust be lessened, and the number of the said Fees so extreamly multiplyed: so as now the profits of such Offices (being become cleer, and the work so easie as any man is capable of it, even those that never saw it,) are bought and sold for Years or Lives, as any other Annuity may be; and withal, the splendor arising from the easie gaines of those places in Courts of Justice, is called the Flourishing of the Law, which certainly flourisheth best, when the Professors and Ministers of it have least to do. And moreover, when the burthen and uselesness of such an Office is taken notice of, 'tis nevertheless spared as a Subjects Freehold in favour of him that bought it.

Of these Offices are many in this Nation, and such as might be a Revenue to the King, either by their Annual profits, or the Sale of them for many years together. And these are the Offices that are properly Saleable, *viz.* where the Fees are large, as appointed when the number of them was few, and also numerous, as multiplying upon the increase of business, and where the business is onely the labour of the meanest men: length of time having made all the work so easie, and found out security against all the frauds, breaches of trust, and male-administrations, whereunto the infancies of those places were obnoxious.

These Offices are therefore Taxes upon such as can or will not avoid the passing through them, and are born as men endure and run themselves into the mischiefs of Duelling, the which are very great, which side soever prevails; for certainly men do not always go to Law to obtain right, or prevent wrong, which judicious neighbours might perform as well as a Jury of no abler men; and men might tell the Judge himself the merits of their Cause, as well as now they instruct their Councel. This therefore of Offices is a voluntary Tax upon contentious men, as Excize upon Drink is, to good Fellows to love it.

CHAPTER. XII.

Of Tythes.

The Word Tythes being the same with Tenths, signifie of it self no more then the proportion of the Excisum, or part retrenched, as if Customs upon imported and exported Commodities should be called by the name of Twentieths, as it is sometimes called Tunnage and Poundage; wherefore it remains to say, that Tythes in this place, do together with the said proportion, consignifie the use of it, *viz.* the maintenance of the Clergy, as also the matter or substance out of which this Maintenance is cut, *viz.* the immediate fruit of the Land and Waters, or the proceed of mens Labour, Art, and Stock laid out upon them. It signifies also the manner of paying it, *viz.* in *specie*, and not (but upon special and voluntary causes) in money.

2. We said the matter of Tythes, was the immediate Fruits of the Earth, *viz.* of Grain as soon as 'tis ready to be removed from the ground that bare it; and not of Bread which is Corn thresht, winnowed, ground, tempered with liquor and baked.

3. 'Tis also the second choice out of the young of multiparous Cattle taken in *specie*, so soon as the said Younglings can subsist without their Dams, or else a Composition in Money for the Uniparous.

4. 'Tis Wool, so soon as it is shorn; 'tis Fowl and Fish, where Fowling and Fishing is rather a Trade then a meer Recreation, & *sic de cæteris*.

5. Moreover, in great Cities Tythes are a kinde of composition in Money for the labour and profit of the Artisans who work upon the materials which have paid Tythes before.

6. Tythes therefore encrease within any Territory, as the labour of that Countrey increases; and labour doth or ought to increase as the people do; now within four hundred years the people of *England* are about quadrupled, as doubling every two hundred years, and the proportion of the Rent of all the Lands in *England* is about the fourth part of the Expence of the people in it, so as the other three parts is labour and stock.

7. Wherefore the Tythes now should be twelve times as good as they were four hundred years ago; which the rates of Benefices in the Kings books do pretty well shew, by comparing of times; something of this should be abated because the proportion between the proceed of Lands and Labour do vary as the hands of Labourers vary: Wherefore we shall rather say, that the Tythes are but six times as good now as four hundred years ago, that is, that the Tythes now would pay six times as many Labourers, or feed six times as many mouthes, as the Tythes four hundred years ago would have done.

8. Now if there were not onely as many Parishes then as now, more Priests in every Parish, and also more Religious Men who were also Priests, and the Religion of those times being more operose, and fuller of work then now, by reason of Confessions, Holydayes, Offices, &c. more in those dayes then now, (the great work in these dayes being a compendious teaching above a thousand at once without much particular Confession and Catechising, or trouble about the Dead), it seems clear, that the Clergy now is far richer then heretofore; and that to be a Clergy-man then was a kinde of a Mortification, whereas now (praised be God) 'tis matter of splendour and magnificence; unless any will say, that there were golden Priests when the Chalices were wood, and but wooden Priests when the Chalices were gold; or that Religion best flourisheth when the Priests are most mortified, as was before said of the Law, which best flourisheth when Lawyers have least to do.

9. But what ever the increase of the Churches Goods are, I grudge it them not; onely wish, that they would take a course to enjoy it with safety and peace to themselves; whereof one is, not to breed more Churchmen then the Benefices as they now stand shared out, will receive; that is to say, if there be places but for about twelve thousand in *England* and *Wales*, it will not be safe to breed up 24000. Ministers, upon a view or conceipt that the Church means otherwise distributed might suffice them all; for then the twelve thousand which are unprovided for, will seek wayes how to get themselves a livelihood; which they cannot do more easily then by perswading the people, that the twelve thousand Incumbents do poison or starve their souls, and misguide them in their way to Heaven: Which needy men upon a strong temptation will do effectually; we having observed, that Lecturers being such a sort of Supernumeraries, have preached more times in a week, more hours in the day, and with greater vehemence every time then the Incumbents could afford to do; for *Graculus esuriens in Cælum, jusseris, ibit.* Now this vehemence, this pains, this zeal, and this living upon particular donations, makes the people think, that those who act them are withall more Orthodox, nay better assisted from God then the others. Now let any man judge, whether men reputed to be inspired will not get help to lift themselves into Church-livings, &c. But these things are too plain from the latest experiences.

10. Now you will ask, how shall that be done, or how may we know how to adjust our Nursery to our Orchard? To which I answer, that if there be twelve thousand Church-livings in *England*, Dignitaries included, then that about four hundred being sent forth *per ann.* into the Vineyard, may keep it well served, without luxuriency; for according to the Mortality-Bill-observation, about that number will dye yearly out of twelve thousand Adult-persons, such as Ministers are as to age, and ought to be as well as to speculative knowledge, as practical experience, both of themselves and others.

11. But I have digressed, my main scope being to explain the nature of the Tax of Tythes; nevertheless since the end of such explanation is but to perswade men to bear quietly so much Tax as is necessary, and not to kick against the pricks; and since the end of that again, and the end of all else we are to do, is but to preserve the publick Peace, I think I have not been impertinent in inserting this little Advertisement, making so much for the Peace of our *Jerusalem*.

12. But to return to Tythes as a Tax or Levy, I say that in *England* it is none, whatsoever it might be or seem to be in the first Age of its Institution; nor will the Kings Quit-rents in *Ireland* as they are properly none now, seem any in the next Age, when every man will proportion his Expence to the remainder of his own Rent after the King is paid his; for 'tis surprize and the suddenness of the Charge, which a Tax supervenient to a mans other expences and issues makes, that renders it a burthen, and that intolerable to such as will not understand it, making men even to take up Arms to withstand it; that is, leap out of the Frying-pan upon earth into the fire even of hell, which is War and the consequences thereof.

13. Now Tythes being no Tax, I speak of it but as the *modus* or pattern of a Tax, affirming it to be next to one, the most equal and indifferent which can be appointed in order to defray the publick Charge of the whole Nation as well as that of the Church; for hereby is collected a proportion of all the Corn, Cattle, Fish, Fowl, Fruit, Wool, Honey, Wax, Oyl, Hemp, and Flax of the Nation, as a result of the Lands, Art, Labour, and Stock which produced them; onely it is scarce regular in respect of Housing, Cloth, Drinks, Leather, Feathers, and the several Manufactures of them; insomuch, as if the difference of Tythes which the Countrey payes in proportion to the City, were now *de novo* to be established, I do not see what in likelihood would sooner cause a grand sedition about it.

14. The payment of an *aliquot* part to the King out of the same things as now pay Tythes, *in specie*, would have an inconvenience, because the Kings Rents would be like the Dividend in Colledges, *viz.* higher or lower according to the prices of those Commodities, unless the said inequality in Colledges happen by reason of the fewness of particulars, according to the market rates whereof, their Rents are paid in money; whereas the whole of all the particulars might well enough ballance each other, a dear or plentiful year being but an appellation *secundum quid*, *viz.* with reference as to Corn onely, as the chief food of the multitude; whereas 'tis likely, that the same causes which makes Corn scarce may make other things in plenty of no less use to the King; as repairing in one thing what he wants in another.

15. Another inconvenience would be that which was observed in *Ireland*, when the Ministry were paid by Sallary, and the Tythes in kinde paid to the

State; who because they could not actually receive them *in specie*, let them at farm to the most bidder; in the Transaction whereof was much juggling, combination, and collusion, which perhaps might have been remedied, had not that course been used but as a sudden temporary shift, without intention of continuing it.

16. The third inconvenience is, that abovementioned, *viz.* the necessity of another way of Tax, to take in the Manufactures of those Commodities which pay the Tax of Tythes; whereas possibly there is a way of Tax equal in its own nature, and which needs not to be pieced up by any other; so as the Officers about that may have a full employment, and none others wanted, whose wide intervals of leasure shall make them seem Drones, as they are also the Caterpillers of any State.

CHAPTER. XIII.

Of several smaller wayes of levying Money.

When the people are weary of any one sort of Tax, presently some Projector propounds another, and gets himself audience, by affirming he can propound a way how all the publick charge may be born without the way that is. As for example, if a Land-tax be the present distasted way, and the people weary of it, then he offers to do the business without such a Land-tax, and propound either a Poll-money, Excize, or the institution of some new Office or Monopoly, and hereby draws some or other to hearken to him; which is readily enough done by those who are not in the places of profit relating to the way of Levies in use, but hope to make themselves Offices in the new Institution.

2. I shall enumerate a few of the smaller wayes which I have observed in several places of *Europe*, *viz*.

First, in some places the State is common Cashier for all or most moneys, as where Banks are, thereby gaining the interest of as much money as is deposited in their hands.

Secondly, Sometimes the State is the common Usurer, as where Loan Banks, and *montes pietatis* are in use, and might be more copiously and effectually where Registers of Lands are kept.

Thirdly, Sometimes the State is or may be Common Ensurer, either upon the danger onely of Enemies at sea, according to the supposed primitive end of our Customs in *England*, or else of the casualties of the Enemy, Weather, Sea, and Vessel taken together.

Fourthly, Sometimes the State hath the whole sale and benefit of certain Commodities, as of Amber in the Duke of *Brandenburghs* Countrey, Tobacco formerly in *Ireland*, Salt in *France*, &c.

Fifthly, Sometimes the State is common Beggar, as 'tis almost in *Holland*, where particular Charity seems only to serve for the relief of concealed wants, and to save these wanting from the shame of discovering their poverty, and not so much to relieve any wants that are declared, and already publickly known.

Sixthly, In some places the State is the sole Guardian of Minors, Lunaticks, and Idiots.

Seventhly, In some other Countreys the State sets up and maintains Play-houses, and publick Entertainments, giving Sallaries to the Actors, but receiving the bulk of the profit to themselves.

Eighthly, In some places, Houses are ensured from fire by the State at a small Rent *per annum* upon each.

Ninthly, In some places Tolls are taken upon passage over Bridges, Causeys, and Ferries built and maintained at the Publick Charge.

Tenthly, In some places men that dye are obliged to leave a certain pittance to the publick, the same is practised in other places upon Marriages, and may be in others upon Births.

Eleventhly, In some places strangers especially Jews, are particularly taxed; which may be good in over-peopled Countreys, though bad in the contrary case.

3. As for Jews, they may well bear somewhat extraordinary, because they seldom eat and drink with Christians, hold it no disparagement to live frugally, and even sordidly among themselves, by which way alone they become able to under-sell any other Traders, to elude the Excize, which bears but according to mens Expences; as also other Duties, by dealing so much in Bills of Exchange, Jewels, and Money, and by practising of several frauds with more impunity then others; for by their being at home every where, and yet no where they become responsible almost for nothing.

4. Twelfthly, There have been in our times, wayes of levying an *aliquot* part of mens Estates, as a Fifth, and Twentieth, *viz.* of their Estates real and personal, yea of their Offices, Faculties, and imaginary Estates also, in and about which way may be so much fraud, collusion, oppression, and trouble, some purposely getting themselves taxed to gain more trust: Others bribing to be taxed low, and it being impossible to check or examine, or trace these Collections by the print of any footsteps they leave, (such as the Harths of Chimneys are) that I have not patience to speak more against it; daring rather conclude without more ado, in the words of our Comick to be naught, yea exceeding naught, very abominable, and not good.

CHAPTER. XIV.

Of raising, depressing, or embasing of Money.

Sometimes it hath happened, that States (I know not by what raw advice) have raised or embased their money, hoping thereby, as it were, to multiply it, and make it pass for more then it did before; that is, to purchase more commodity or labour with it: All which indeed and in truth, amounts to no more then a Tax, upon such People unto whom the State is indebted, or a defalkation of what is due; as also the like burthen upon all that live upon Pensions, established Rents, Annuities, Fees, Gratuities, &c.

2. To explain this fully, one might lanch out into the deep Ocean of all the Mysteries concerning Money, which is done for other ends elsewhere; nevertheless I shall do it the best I can, by expounding the reasons *pro & contrà* for embasing and raising of Money: and first of embasing.

3. Copper or Tin Money made *ad valorem* in its matter, is no embasing; the same being onely cumbersom and baser then silver money, onely because less convenient and portable.

And Copper money *ad valorem* in workmanship and matter both together; (such as on which the Effigies and Scutcheon are so curiously graven and impressed, as the moneys seem rather Medalls) is not embasing, unless the numbers of such pieces be excessive, (the measures whereof I shall not set down, until I shall hereafter propound the fittest Sections of the abstracted pound into which I would have money coyned, and determine how many pieces of each Section should be in an hundred pound) for in case of such excess, the workmanship being of no other use but to look upon, becomes base by its being too common.

4. Nor are such Tokens base as are coyned for Exchange in retailing by particular men, (if such men be responsible and able to take them back, and give Silver for them.)

5. But that Gold I count to be embased, which hath more allay either of Copper or Silver in it, then serves to correct its too great natural softness and flexibility, whereby it wears too fast in Money: And that Silver I reckon also embased, wherein is commixed more Copper then will sufficiently toughen it, and save it from cracking under the Hammer, Press, or Mill that must coin it, or the like.

6. Base Money is therefore such as Dutch Shillings, Stivers, French Soulz, Irish Bon-galls, &c. and for the most part consisting of great pieces, though

of small value. To answer the first reason or pretence of making them, which is, that the said Pieces might be more bulky, handleable, and the silver in them less apt to be lost or worn away.

7. The other reason (besides that of allay which we must allow in the Measures abovementioned) is to save it from being melted down by Goldsmiths and Bullioners, or exported by strangers; neither of which can happen but to their loss: for suppose a Stiver of two pence, had a penny of pure silver, if the Bullioner melts it for the sake of the silver onely, in the separation he shall lose the Copper and charge of refining the Silver; nor will strangers export it into places where the local value of the Piece perisheth, the intrinsick leaving him to loss.

7. Now the reasons against this kinde of Money are, first the greater danger of falsification, because the colour, sound, and weight by which men (without the test) guess at the goodness of the material of Money is too much confounded, for the vulgar (whom it concerns) to make use of them for their marks and guides in the business.

8. Secondly, In case small pieces of this Money, *viz.* pieces of two pence should happen to be raised or depressed twelve, fifteen, or sixteen *per cent.* then there will be a certain loss by reason of the fractions, which the vulgar cannot reckon: As for example, if such Money were depressed but ten, eleven, or twelve *per cent.* then the two pence piece would be worth but three half pence, which is twenty five *per cent.* and so of other proportions.

9. Thirdly, In case the Inconvenience of this Money should be so great as to necessitate a new Coinage of it, then will happen all the losses we mentioned before in melting it down by Bullioners.

10. Fourthly, If the two pence piece contained but **1. 5.** th. part of the Silver usually in a shilling, then Dealers would have fifteen pence paid in this money for the same Commodity, for which they would take a shilling in Standard Silver.

11. Raising of Money is either the cutting the pound *Troy* of Standard Silver into more pieces then formerly, as into above sixty, whereas heretofore the same was made but into twenty, and yet both sorts called shillings, or else calling the money already made by higher names: The reasons or pretences given for such raising are these, *viz.* That the raising of Money will bring it in, and the material thereof more plentifully; for trial whereof suppose one shilling were proclaimed to be worth two, what other effect could this have, then the raising of all Commodities unto a double price? Now if it were proclaimed, That Labourers Wages, &c. should not rise at all upon this raising of Money, then would this Act be as onely a Tax upon the said

Labourers, as forcing them to lose half their wages, which would not be onely unjust but impossible, unless they could live with the said half, (which is not to be supposed) for then the Law that appoints such Wages were ill made, which should allow the Labourer but just wherewithall to live; for if you allow double, then he works but half so much as he could have done, and otherwise would; which is a loss to the Publick of the fruit of so much labour.

12. But suppose the *Quart d' Ecus* of *France* commonly esteemed worth eighteen pence were raised to three shillings, then 'tis true, that all the Moneys of *England* would be indeed *Quart d' Ecus* pieces; but as true, that all the English Money would be carried away, and that our *Quart d' Ecus* would contain but half so much Bullion as our own money did; so that raising of Money may indeed change the *species*, but with so much loss as the Forreign Pieces were raised unto, above their intrinsick value.

13. But for remedy of this, suppose we raised the *Quart d' Ecus* double, and prohibited the Exportation of our own money in Exchange thereof. I answer, that such a Prohibition is nugatory, and impossible to be executed; and if it were not, yet the raising of the said *species* would but make us sell the Commodities bought with raised *Quart d' Ecus*, in effect but at half the usual rate, which unto them that want such commodities will as well yield the full; so that abating our prices, will as well allure strangers to buy extraordinary proportions of our Commodities, as raising their money will do: But neither that, nor abating the price will make strangers use more of our Commodities then they want; for although the first year they should carry away an unuseful and superfluous proportion, yet afterwards they would take so much the less.

14. If this be true, as in substance it is, why then have so many wise States in several ancient, as well as modern times frequently practised this Artifice, as a means to draw in money into their respective Dominions?

I answer, that something is to be attributed to the stupidity and ignorance of the people, who cannot of a sudden understand this matter: for I finde many men wise enough, who though they be well informed that raising of money signifies little, yet cannot suddenly digest it. As for example, an unengaged person who had money in his purse in *England*, and should hear that a shilling was made fourteen pence in *Ireland*, would more readily run thither to buy Land then before; not suddenly apprehending, that for the same Land which he might have bought before for six years Purchase, he shall now pay seven. Nor will Sellers in *Ireland* of a sudden apprehend cause to raise their Land proportionally, but will at least be contented to compound the business, *viz*. to sell at six and an half; and if the difference be a more ragged fraction, men under a long time will not apprehend it, nor ever be able exactly to govern their practice according to it.

15. Secondly, Although I apprehend little real difference between raising Forreign Money to double, and abating half in the price of our own Commodities, yet to sell them on a tacite condition to be paid in Forreign present Money, shall increase our money; forasmuch as between raising the money, and abasing the price, is the same difference as between selling for money and in barter, which latter is the dearer; or between selling for present money, and for time; barter resolving into the nature of uncertain time.

16. I say, suppose English Cloth were sold at six shillings a Yard, and French Canvas at eighteen pence the Ell, the question is, whether it were all one in order to increase Money in *England* to raise the French Money double, or to abate half of the price of our Cloth? I think the former better, because that former way or proposition carries with it a condition of having Forreign Money in *specie*, and not Canvas in barter, between which two wayes the world generally agrees there is a difference. Wherefore if we can afford to abate half our price, but will not do it but for our neighbours money, then we gain so much as the said difference between Money and Barter amounts unto, by such raising of our Neighbours Money.

17. But the fundamental solution of this Question depends upon a real and not an imaginary way of computing the prices of Commodities; in order to which real way I premise these suppositions: First then, suppose there be in a Territory a thousand people, let these people be supposed sufficient to Till this whole Territory as to the Husbandry of Corn, which we will suppose to contain all necessaries for life, as in the Lords Prayer we suppose the word Bread doth; and let the production of a Bushel of this Corn be supposed of equal labour to that of producing an ounce of Silver. Suppose again that a tenth part of this Land, and tenth of the people, viz. an hundred of them, can produce Corn enough for the whole; suppose that the Rent of Land (found out as abovementioned) be a fourth part of the whole product, (about which proportion it really is, as we may perceive by paying a fourth Sheaf instead of Rent in some places) suppose also that whereas but an hundred are necessary for this Husbandry, yet that two hundred have taken up the Trade; and suppose that where a Bushel of Corn would suffice, yet men out of delicacy will use two, making use of the Flower onely of both. Now the Inferences from hence are;

First, That the goodness or badness, or the value of Land depends upon the greater or lesser share of the product given for it in proportion to the simple labour bestowed to raise the said Product.

Secondly, That the proportions between Corn and Silver signifie onely an artificial value, not a natural; because the comparison is between a thing naturally useful, and a thing in it self unnecessary, which (by the way) is part of the reason why there are not so great changes and leaps in the prices of Silver as of other Commodities.

Thirdly, That natural dearness and cheapness depends upon the few or more hands requisite to necessaries of Nature: As Corn is cheaper where one man produces Corn for ten, then where he can do the like but for six; and withall, according as the Climate disposes men to a necessity of spending more or less. But Political Cheapness depends upon the paucity of Supernumerary Interlopers into any Trade over and above all that are necessary, *viz.* Corn will be twice as dear where are two hundred Husbandmen to do the same work which an hundred could perform: the proportion thereof being compounded with the proportion of superfluous Expence, (*viz.* if to the cause of dearness abovementioned be added to the double Expence to what is necessary) then the natural price will appear quadrupled; and this quadruple Price is the true Political Price computed upon naturall grounds.

And this again proportioned to the common artificiall Standard Silver gives what was sought; that is, the true Price Currant.

18. But forasmuch as almost all Commodities have their Substitutes or Succedanea, and that almost all uses may be answered several wayes; and for that novelty, surprize, example of Superiours, and opinion of unexaminable effects do adde or take away from the price of things, we must adde these contingent Causes to the permanent Causes abovementioned, in the judicious foresight and computation whereof lies the excellency of a Merchant.

Now to apply this Digression, I say, that to encrease Money, it is as well necessary to know how to abate as raise, the price of Commodities, and that of Money, which was the scope of the said Digression.

19. To conclude this whole Chapter, we say, that raising or embasing of Moneys is a very pittiful and unequal way of Taxing the people; and 'tis a sign that the State sinketh, which catcheth hold on such Weeds as are accompanied with the dishonour of impressing a Princes Effigies to justifie Adulterate Commodities, and the breach of Publick Faith, such as is the calling a thing what it really is not.

CHAPTER. XV.

Of Excize.

It is generally allowed by all, that men should contribute to the Publick Charge but according to the share and interest they have in the Publick Peace; that is, according to their Estates or Riches: now there are two sorts of Riches, one actual, and the other potential. A man is actually and truly rich according to what he eateth, drinketh, weareth, or any other way really and actually enjoyeth; others are but potentially or imaginatively rich, who though they have power overmuch, make little use of it; these being rather Stewards and Exchangers for the other sort, then owners for themselves.

2. Concluding therefore that every man ought to contribute according to what he taketh to himself, and actually enjoyeth. The first thing to be done is, to compute what the Total of the Expence of this Nation is by particular men upon themselves, and then what part thereof is necessary for the Publick; both which (no not the former) are so difficult as most men imagine.

3. In the next place we must conceive, that the very perfect Idea of making a Leavy upon Consumptions, is to rate every particular Necessary, just when it is ripe for Consumption; that is to say, not to rate Corn until it be Bread, nor Wool until it be Cloth, or rather until it be a very Garment; so as the value of Wool, Cloathing, and Tayloring, even to the Thread and Needles might be comprehended; But this being perhaps too laborious to be performed, we ought to enumerate a Catalogue of Commodities both native and artificial, such whereof accompts may be most easily taken, and can bear the Office marks either on themselves, or on what contains them; being withall such, as are to be as near Consumption as possible: And then we are to compute what further labour or charge is to be bestowed on each of them, before consumption, that so an allowance be given accordingly. As for example, suppose there be an hundred pounds worth of Stript Stuff for Hangings, and an hundred pounds worth of Cloth or Stuff for the best mens Cloathes; I conceive, that the Cloth should bear a greater Excize then the said stript stuff, the one wanting nothing but tacking up, to be at its wayes end; and the other Tayloring, Thread, Silk, Needles, Thimbles, Buttons, and several other particulars: The Excise of all which must be accumulated upon the Excize of the Cloth, unless they be so great (as perhaps Buttons, Lace, or Ribbons may be) to be taxed apart, and inserted into the Catalogue abovementioned.

4. Now the things to be accumulated upon Cloth are, as near as possible, to be such particulars as are used onely to Cloth, or very rarely to any other particular, as the several sorts of peculiar trimmings; so on Corn should be accumulated the charge of grinding, bolting, yeast, &c. for the baking of it

into Bread, unless, as was said before, any of these particulars can be better rated apart.

5. A Question ariseth hence, whether any Native Commodities exported ought to pay the Excize, or that what is imported in lieu of it should pay none? I answer no, because they are not spent here *in specie*; but I conceive that the Goods returned from abroad for them and spent here should pay, if the exported have not already, for so shall what we spend pay once, but not oftner. Now if Bullion be returned, then if it be coyned into Money it ought not to pay, because Money will beget other commodities which shall pay; but if the said Bullion be wrought into Plate and Utensils, or disgrost into Wire or Lace, or beaten into Fueilles, then it also ought to pay, because it is consumed and absolutely spent, as in Lace and Gilding is too notorious; and this is the reason why I think the Leavy we commonly call Customs to be unseasonable and preposterous, the same being a payment before consumption.

6. We have several times spoken of Accumulative Excize, by which we mean Taxing many things together as one: As for example, suppose the many Drugs used in Treacle or Mithridate were used onely in those Compositions, in such case by taxing any one of them, the whole number will be taxed as certainly as that one, because they all bear a certain proportion one to another: In Cloth, the Workmanship and Tools as well as the Wool may be well enough taxed, &c.

7. But some have strained this Accumulation so, as they would have all things together taxed upon some one single particular, such as they think to be nearest the Common Standard of all Expence, the principal ends of their proposition being these, *viz.*

First, To disguise the name of Excize, as odious to them, that do neither know the payment of Taxes to be as indispensable as eating, and as have not considered the natural justice of this way of Excizing or proportionating.

Secondly, To avoid the trouble and charge of Collecting.

Thirdly, To bring the business *ad firmum*, and to a certainty of all which we shall speak hereafter, when we examine the several reasons for and against the way of Excize, proceeding now to the several *species* of Accumulative Excizes propounded in the world.

8. Some propound Beer to be the only Excizable Commodity, supposing that in the proportion that men drink, they make all other Expences; which certainly will not hold, especially if Strong Beer pay quintuple unto, (as now) or any more Excize then the small: For poor Carpenters, Smiths, Feltmakers, &c. drinking twice as much Strong Beer as Gentlemen do of Small, must consequently pay ten times as much Excize. Moreover, upon the Artizans

Beer is accumulated, onely a little Bread and Cheese, leathern Clothes, Neck-Beef, and Inwards twice a week, stale Fish, old Pease without Butter, &c. Whereas on the other, beside Drink, is accumulated as many more things as Nature and Art can produce; besides this way of Excizing, though it be never so well administred, is neither so equal nor so easie, nor so examinable as the simple Poll-money before spoken of, which is also but an Accumulative Excize.

9. What hath been propounded for Beer may be of Salt, Fuel, Bread, &c. and the Propositions would all labour under the same Inconveniences; for some spend more, some less of these Commodities; and sometimes Families (each whereof are propounded to be farmed, without descending to individual heads) are more numerous at sometimes then at others, according as their Estates or other Interests shall wax or wane.

10. Of all the Accumulative Excizes, that of Harth-money or Smoak-money seems the best; and that onely because the easiest, and clearest, and fittest to ground a certain Revenue upon; it being easie to tell the number of Harths, which remove not as Heads or Polls do: Moreover, 'tis more easie to pay a small Tax, then to alter or abrogate Harths, even though they are useless and supernumerary; nor is it possible to cover them, because most of the neighbours know them; nor in new Building will any man who gives forty shillings for making a Chimney be without it for two.

11. Here is to be noted, that a Harth-money must be but small, or else 'twill be intolerable; it being more easie for a Gentleman of a thousand pound *per annum* to pay for an hundred Chimneys (few of their Mansion-Houses having more) then for Labourers to pay for two. Moreover, if the Land-Lord onely pay this Tax, then is it not an Accumulative Excize for all, but a particular Excize upon but one onely Commodity, namely Housing.

12. Now the Reasons for Excize are these, *viz.*

First, The Natural Justice that every man should pay according to what he actually enjoyeth; upon which account this Tax is scarce forced upon any, and is very light to those, who please to be content with natural Necessaries.

Secondly, This Tax if it be not farmed, but regularly collected, engages to thrift, the onely way to enrich a Nation, as by the Dutch and Jews, and by all other men, who have come to vaste Estates by Trade, doth appear.

Thirdly, No man payes double or twice for the same thing, forasmuch as nothing can be spent but once; whereas it is frequently seen, that otherwise men pay both by the Rent of their Lands, by their Smoaks, by their Titles, and by Customs, (which all men do, though Merchants chiefly talk of it) they also pay by Benevolence and by Tythes; whereas in this way of Excize no man need pay but one way, nor but once, properly speaking.

Fifthly, By this way an excellent account may be taken of the Wealth, Growth, Trade, and strength of the Nation at all times. All which Reasons do make not for particular compoundings with Families, nor for letting the whole to farm, but for collecting it by special Officers, who having a full employment, will not be a fourth of the charge of our present many multiform Levies; for to put extraordinary trouble and hazzard upon the Countrey Officers, is a sorer Taxing of them, then to make them pay a small Reward unto practised Persons to be their Substitutes. All which are the common Objections against Excize.

13. I should here adde the manner of Collecting it, but I refer this to the practice of *Holland*; and I might also offer how men may be framed to be fit for this and other Publick Trusts, as to be Cashiers, Store-keepers, Collectors, &c. but I refer this Enquiry unto a more ample and fit occasion.

Milton Keynes UK
Ingram Content Group UK Ltd.
UKHW031349260824
447288UK00013B/212